Lift
Every
Voice
and
Sing
II

An
African
American
Hymnal

Lift Every Voice and Sing II

An African American Hymnal

 CHURCH

CHURCH PUBLISHING INCORPORATED, NEW YORK

Canon 24, Section 1

It shall be the duty of every Minister to see that music is used as an offering for the glory of God and as a help to the people in their worship in accordance with The Book of Common Prayer and as authorized by the rubrics or by the General Convention of this Church. To this end the Minister shall have final authority in the administration of matters pertaining to music. In fulfilling this responsibility the Minister shall seek assistance from persons skilled in music. Together they shall see that music is appropriate to the context in which it is used.

20 19 18 17 16 15 14 13

This hymnal
is dedicated to the
memory of

The Reverend

Curtis Winfield Sisco, Jr.

1958 – 1992

creative liturgist
gifted musician
devoted priest

Contents

Preface

At the outset, the Editorial Committee decided that *Lift Every Voice and Sing II* would contain music drawn from the following genres:

Negro spirituals
Traditional and contemporary Gospel songs
Adapted Protestant hymns
Missionary and evangelistic hymns
Service music and mass settings in both
traditional and Gospel settings

It was later decided to include a section containing hymns for African American saints on the Church's calendar.

The contents of the hymnal were drawn from several sources. The committee chose hymns to be retained from *LEVAS I* and hymns from other black hymnals. Notably, *"Lead Me, Guide Me"* (Roman Catholic) and *"Songs of Zion"* (United Methodist) were consulted as were Caribbean hymnals. Also, since *LEVAS II* is seen to be a supplement to *The Hymnal 1982*, it was decided that with the exception of the "title hymn" and one or two others with unique arrangements, we would not include hymns which are contained in 1982. In addition, it was decided to include several new works (both texts and music) which were subsequently solicited or commissioned.

While the reasons for choosing spirituals and Gospel songs may be obvious, the *raison d'être* for the inclusion of missionary and evangelistic hymns and "adapted Protestant hymns" might need some explanation. Bishop Burgess, in his Preface to *LEVAS I,* observed:

Just as the slaves not only adopted the religion of their masters, but transformed it into a Gospel that had particular meaning for themselves, so the Black Christians have taken the hymnody of the evangelical church and claimed it for their own. These hymns do not have the theological purity of the spirituals, nor do they arise out of the bitter experience of Black people. In adopting this music, again like the Christian religion itself, the Black congregation has used the notation merely as a guide. The free expression of enthusiastic faith has raised this music into a genre that rightly takes its place within Black congregational worship.

The Committee was especially interested in providing mass settings and service music reflective of the black musical idiom. In a survey conducted by the committee at the beginning of the project, such a need was duly noted, since the paucity of such music was seen as a deficiency of *LEVAS I*. The survey also reminded us that almost all black parishes are Eucharistically-centered. Therefore, the decision was made that service music in *LEVAS II* would include only that used in the Holy Eucharist.

The arrangement of the contents of *LEVAS II* is worthy of comment. We were concerned that we keep in mind that in this church we follow a liturgical year and that hymns be used appropriately. There is a fine art in choosing hymns which are theologically and thematically compatible with the liturgy. Hymns which were not composed originally to fit into a liturgical context were studied to determine where they could best be employed. One result of this is that certain hymns have been rescued from obscurity, and others have been given new significance. This arrangement will help planners of worship use hymns germane to a particular season or occasion.

There are so many individuals to whom we owe thanks. We acknowledge first those who have gone before and succeeded in providing for the Episcopal Church the first collection of African American sacred songs—*Lift Every Voice and Sing I*. Particular thanks is expressed to the Rt. Rev. Franklin D. Turner, now suffragan bishop of Pennsylvania. To him, to the Rt. Rev. John M. Burgess, retired bishop of Massachusetts and to Dr. Irene V. Jackson-Brown is expressed appreciation for their determination to complete the first edition of this hymnal. We stand on their shoulders in continuing the work they began.

Lift Every Voice and Sing II is a new musical resource and would not have been accomplished were it not for the tireless efforts of its gifted Editorial Committee. Therefore to them go primary credit and praise for their hours of work too numerous to count.

We are especially grateful to Dr. Horace Clarence Boyer, Professor of Music at the University of Massachusetts, at Amherst, who served creatively and with distinction as General Editor. Dr. Carl Haywood, Professor of Music at Norfolk State University and organist/choir director at Grace Episcopal Church in Norfolk, Virginia served as editor of the service music section and made incomparable contributions toward the completion of this hymnal. Until his death, the Rev. Curtis W. Sisco, Rector of St. Luke's Church in New Orleans served proficiently as liturgical editor and was of immeasurable value on the Committee.

Every Committee member contributed his or her unique gifts. Therefore profound gratitude is also expressed to Dr. Deborah Harmon Hines, the Rev. Dr. Richard C. Martin, Mr. Robert L. Simpson, Mrs. Doris P. Summey (secretary), and Mrs. Irma Tillery.

The Editorial Committee was ably staffed by the Rev. Canon Harold T. Lewis, of the Office for Black Ministries, by Mr. Frank Hemlin, Publisher of the Church Hymnal Corporation and by Dr. Irene V. Jackson-Brown in her capacity as Coordinator of Program Resources at the Episcopal Church Center.

A word of thanks goes to the members of the Union of Black Episcopalians who through their completion of questionnaires, letters and correspondence assisted the Editorial Committee in selecting materials for this collection.

We thank Mr. Marc S. Jones of the Office for Black Ministries who coordinated the copyright process and Mrs. Margaret West of the Church Hymnal Corporation who oversaw the engraving process. Thanks are due to the Rev. Dr. Kortright Davis and to the Rev. Dr. Lloyd A. Lewis, Jr. who reviewed the words of each hymn for theological clarity and to Dr. Carl G. Harris and Dr. Adolphus Hailstork who reviewed the musical texts. The cover design is the result of the artistry of the gifted Dr. Dwight Johnson.

We are grateful to the Episcopal Commission for Black Ministries, the Standing Commission on Church Music and the Church Hymnal Corporation whose cooperation and support brought this effort to completion.

Finally we are indebted to every composer, arranger and lyricist whose work is represented in this collection of African American sacred songs.

We have completed our work trusting that all we have done is to the glory of God. We join in the words of the Psalmist, *"Sing to the Lord a new song; sing his praise in the congregation of the faithful. Let everything that has breath praise the Lord"*.

The Rt. Rev. Arthur B. Williams, Jr., D.D.
Chair of the Editorial Board
Bishop Suffragan of Ohio

Introduction

Why an African American Hymnal?

The ways in which a people expresses itself musically and liturgically provide us, perhaps, with the most significant insights into its culture. Believing this, and in an attempt to share some of the gifts that black people bring to the whole church, the Episcopal Commission for Black Ministries, under the aegis of the Church Hymnal Corporation, published *Lift Every Voice and Sing: A Collection of Afro-American Spirituals and Other Songs (LEVAS I)* in 1981. Today, a little more than a decade later, in collaboration with the Standing Commission on Church Music, and again under the aegis of the Church Hymnal Corporation, the Episcopal Commission for Black Ministries now offers *Lift Every Voice and Sing II: An African American Hymnal (LEVAS II)*.

While it is not within the scope of this introduction to give a comprehensive overview of church music among black Episcopalians, a few observations might enable us to better understand the place of *LEVAS II* in that historical evolution. There is an old French proverb: *"Plus ça change, plus la même chose."* ("The more things change, the more they remain the same.") This adage seems applicable to the development of church music among black Episcopalians. In an article entitled "Music Among Blacks in the Episcopal Church: Some Preliminary Considerations" which appeared in the *Historical Magazine of the Episcopal Church,* Dr. Irene Jackson-Brown, general editor of *LEVAS I,* writes that in the late eighteenth century, "blacks were . . . beginning to experience musical syncretism within the colonial Church of England. That is, blacks were fusing certain African and African American musical practices with Anglo-American musical practices." She also notes that these "musical practices included the singing of religious folk songs," later to be called spirituals.

The Reverend Professor Robert Bennett of the Episcopal Divinity School, in an article entitled "Black Episcopalians: A History from the Colonial Period to the Present Day," also in the *Historical Magazine*, suggests that at least one spiritual actually originated among black Episcopalians:

> In the south, where the majority of black Episcopalians were to be found and where prior to the Civil War the Bishop of South Carolina claimed more black communicants than white and where black churchmen worshipped in separate galleries or chapels, it was this body which described their plantation Holy Communion services in the spiritual, 'Let us break bread together on our knees.'

After the introduction of the organ, many black congregations enjoyed reputations for excellence in church music. From the choir stalls of such places as St. Thomas', Philadelphia (founded by Absalom Jones); St. Philip's, New York City; St. James', Baltimore; and Calvary Church, Charleston, emanated the sacred strains of psalter and hymnal. It was not uncommon for such congregations, in addition to liturgical music, to offer afternoon and evening concerts featuring anthems and other choral works of great composers. But the works chosen were almost always European in origin. A Swedish visitor who attended a service in a black congregation in 1850, included the following comments in a letter home (and I would add parenthetically that the same observations could have been made in 1950):

> I had in the forenoon visited a negro . . . church belonging to the Episcopal creed. There were but few present, and they were of the negro aristocracy of the city. The mode of conducting the divine service was quiet, very proper, and a little tedious. The hymns were beautifully and exquisitely sung.

We must keep in mind that prior to the Civil Rights Movement of the last generation, "black" was often considered not beautiful at all. Celebrating black heritage was not always understood as the way to success in a society in which the dominant culture established the standards to be equalled or excelled. If this was true in society in general, it was no less operative in the church, and in the Episcopal Church in particular. Thus, Bishop Turner, in his Introduction to *LEVAS I*, could write:

> Unfortunately, Afro-Americans, particularly those in predominantly white churches, have not felt comfortable using their own music in formal church services, but instead relegated this music to use at civil and social gatherings. Although Black Episcopalians could not or would not use spirituals in their formal worship, they constantly hummed and sang these songs in private.

The Civil Rights Movement, it can be argued, gave black Episcopalians the license to reclaim the outward and visible signs of their black heritage; and once again, like their forbears of the colonial era, they began to syncretise the clipped cadences of English church music and the syncopations, improvisations and coloratura of the black musical medium. The Venerable Hartshorn Murphy, Archdeacon of Los Angeles, in his keynote address entitled "Expanding our Horizons through Evangelism", delivered at the national conference of the Union of Black Episcopalians in 1989, put it this way:

> As a result of the civil rights and black consciousness movements, something remarkable happened . . . We as a people, re-discovered the validity of "emotionalism" as a religious expression. Where previously, [black] church ladies in the Episcopal Church would go home on Sunday, remove their veils and gloves and sing and listen to spirituals and gospel music, today, they want to do that in church, at least occasionally.

To be sure, this conversion experience was not a universal phenomenon among black Episcopalians. Black Episcopal congregations, like the church at large, number among their members several converts, who often associated the hymns contained in *LEVAS* with music in their former denominational affiliations. But more and more, spirituals, gospel music and mass settings reflective of the black religious experience are enjoying increased prominence, even in those parishes which in a former age, would have limited its mass settings to Willan and Oldroyd, and whose concerts would have featured Vivaldi's "Gloria" or Stainer's "Crucifixion." More correctly, what is happening now is that these parishes are discovering that they can have their liturgical cake and eat it; they can skillfully blend these various elements into a tasteful and artistic whole; like blacks in the colonial era, they have learned to "syncretise." *"Plus ça change, plus la même chose."*

But clearly, *LEVAS II* is not being published solely to enable previously stuffy black Episcopalians to become "sanctified" ones. It is intended to be a resource for the whole church. For as Archdeacon Murphy observes:

> White people, too, want to rejoice and sing "Blessed Assurance" with abandon. This is especially true of young white children who can't get with the program on Sunday mornings after rocking out to Michael Jackson or Whitney Houston all week.

Faithful to the Episcopal Church's new appreciation of multicultural-ism, *The Hymnal 1982,* for which *LEVAS II* will serve as a supplement, is a far more inclusive and representative resource than its predecessor. African, Caribbean, Native American, Hispanic, African-American and other sources have been used, to remind worshippers of the rich diver-sity of all the people of God. We are pleased that the church's official hymnal includes music, both old and new, reflective of the African American experience, and it is in the spirit of providing additional resources from the black musical experience that *LEVAS II* is offered to the Episcopal church at large as well as to our brothers and sisters in the broader ecumenical community. In so doing, we echo the wish of Bishop Burgess, in the Preface to *LEVAS I:*

> It is the hope of the editors and the Commission for Black Ministries that there will be acceptance far beyond those parishes composed largely of Black people. This music will serve the whole church well, if, in making it its own, it will come to understand something more of the mission of all people in today's world.

The history and theology of the black church are embodied in its music. The music of the black church, then, is the expression of the struggle, the pilgrimage and the joy of a people. In an age in which all members of the church are searching for a renewed sense of spirituality, it seems altogether fitting and proper to look to the music of a people whose religious folk songs are for good reason called spirituals. I commend to you the riches of the black musical experience, and express the hope that together we may LIFT EVERY VOICE AND SING!

The Reverend Canon Harold T. Lewis, D.D.
Staff Officer for Black Ministries

Hymns and Songs:
Performance Notes

The African American religious singing tradition is derived principally from musical practices in Africa, the United States and the Caribbean, and therefore incorporates many and diverse songs and styles. The revised *Lift Every Voice and Sing* reflects this musical diversity through the inclusion of several types of songs. While many of these songs, such as standard Protestant hymns, African and Caribbean songs, "Lift Every Voice and Sing" and "Prayer for Africa" are usually performed as written, others, such as gospel songs and Negro spirituals, are performed in the traditional African American improvised singing style, and therefore warrant some notes on performance practices.

Since the formation of the Fisk Jubilee Singers in 1871, there have been two styles of singing Negro spirituals. The older style is taken directly from the singing of the slaves, and celebrates the nuances of African American folk music, while the newer style is based on European art music practices. Either style is acceptable, but the styles should not be mixed.

To ensure the most meaningful worship experiences with the music of *Lift Every Voice and Sing,* a discussion of pertinent performance practices is herewith provided for consideration.

Voice

A full, free, and sonorous tone is the hallmark of African American singing; therefore, the singer is encouraged to sing with a fully opened throat. A timid or muted sacred singing style does not necessarily connote piety in the traditional African American service. To be sure, there is a cherished tolerance in the African American community for unusual voices, and a *good* singer, one who sings with sincerity and conviction, is preferable to the singer who possesses a *beautiful* voice, but who sings without conviction.

Congregational singing is the means by which diverse individuals and groups worship the Savior as one committed union, and can provide expression for the deepest yearnings. Much of the congregational singing is executed in the responsorial ("call-and-response") manner between a soloist and congregation. The soloist is usually an experienced singer and will deliver the "call" with firmness and conviction. The congregation should be just as firm in delivering the "response," as each part is of equal importance.

Text

Negro Spirituals and gospel songs are, in part, characterized by very few words in the text, and therefore depend upon repetition to convey their message. Originally necessitated by the inability to read and the casual circumstances under which they were created, spirituals contained only a few words so that they could be learned and performed easily. It is not unusual for a spiritual to have only two different lines of text:

> Oh, bye and bye, bye and bye
> I'm gonna lay down my heavy load.

In addition to the text contained in the printed score, additional words and phrases are often interjected during performance. There is, in African American sacred music, a catalogue of *wandering* couplets and quatrains which are employed when extending the performance of a song or when variety of text is desired. In many cases the selected couplet or quatrain will further the message of the song, though this is not necessarily a qualification for selection. The *spirit* and performance will determine the added texts. Among popular couplets and quatrains are:

> My Lord's done just what He said,
> He healed the sick and raised the dead.

If you cannot sing like angels,
If you cannot preach like Paul,
You can tell the love of Jesus
And say He died for all.

The tradition is so strong that the text in the printed score will often be discarded in favor of a popular couplet or quatrain. This practice has found its way into gospel music, and often only the refrain of the original composition is retained. Standard textual interpolations such as "Oh, Lord," "Yes, Lord," and "Hallelujah" may often precede a line of printed text, but will not interfere with the rhythmic pulse of the song.

Dialect has been retained in many of the spirituals included in the hymnal, which necessitates a word of caution. Dialect should never be emphasized nor delivered with more force than other words in the text. "De" (the) is pronounced as written before words beginning with vowels, while it is pronounced as "duh" when used before words beginning with consonants. Sometimes words are shortened to accommodate rhythmic pulses, and at other times extended to lengthen the value of a note. In no case should the singer attempt to correct the language.

While most Negro Spirituals refer to "we" and "us," many gospel songs use "I" and "me." The use of the first person pronoun does not exclude the community, but speaks for the community from the vantage of individual piety.

Melody

Melodies in many Negro Spirituals and gospel songs are set to five tones (pentatonic) or fewer. Others employ the diatonic (seven tone) scale, but with the flatted third, sixth or seventh. These melodies should not be corrected to conform to the diatonic scale, but should be celebrated for their economy and variety. The novice singer may experience some concern when a flatted seventh is accompanied by a diatonic seventh. This soft dissonance is part of the musical fabric of African Americans and can be accommodated with a little practice.

When the spirit of a worship service is especially intense, singers will often embellish (improvise) the melody with additional tones, resulting in an expanded melodic line (see Improvisation below).

Harmony

When accompanied by a chordal instrument, African American folk music employs standard Western European tertian (in thirds) harmony. In *a cappella* singing, however, two additional types of harmony are prominent. The first is *parallel* harmony in which the melody is harmonized by a tone at the interval or a third or sixth, with this intervallic relationship remaining constant throughout the performance of the song. This method of harmonizing does not include contrary and oblique motion, so prominent in western music. The second type of additional harmony is reminiscent of Western European organum of the ninth century, in that intervals of the fourth and fifth are in abundance, while thirds and sixths, the basis of modern music, are rare. Such harmony is usually employed when songs are performed at very slow tempos.

There are very few instances when Negro Spirituals and gospel songs are not sung in harmony, and singers are encouraged to create their own harmony when that printed in the score is not easily singable.

Rhythm

The most distinguishing characteristic of African American music is rhythm, and is no less so in sacred singing. Each beat should be clearly articulated and attacked with authority, accenting the principal pulse in a unit stronger than the others. In other instances the weak beats should be given a stronger accent than the primary and secondary pulses:

1   2   3   4

This is especially necessary when singing in a moderately fast tempo, as foot patting (see below) usually takes place on strong beats, leaving weak beats without accents.

Placing the accent on weak rather than strong beats is a feature of syncopation, in which the accent is removed from strong to weak beats, or any portion of a beat except the beginning. Syncopation should never be rushed, but executed solidly within the pulse, and with heavy accentuation. Rushing or anticipating syncopation will cause an increase in the tempo. It is therefore necessary to maintain a clear sense of where the pulse lies so that the combination of the two will create the cross rhythm desired.

Experienced singers often employ symmetrical and asymmetrical divisions of the beat as rhythmic counterpoint to the established pulse. The inexperienced singer should maintain the basic rhythm in such situations, as the resultant rhythm will be one of intricacy and complexity, characteristic of African rhythm.

Meter and Tempo

Standard meters, such as 4/4, 2/4 and 3/4 have been employed for most of the songs in the hymnal, and should be performed in the standard manner. Gospel songs, on the other hand, very often employ a meter involving multiples of three. Therefore, regardless of the meter signature assigned, moderately slow and slow gospel songs should be performed in 6/8, 9/8 or 12/8. This means, for example, a song assigned a meter signature of 4/4 should be performed in 12/8 by allotting three pulses to each quarter note. "Come, Ye Disconsolate" is assigned a meter signature of 4/4:

Come, ye dis - con - so - late

When performed as a gospel song, it should be executed as:

Come, ye dis - con - so - late

Tempo markings have not been indicated in the hymnal, though time and tradition have dictated the tempos at which most of the songs are to be performed. Many of the songs in the hymnal are classified according to tempo, and were assigned tempos when they were created. Negro Spirituals are divided into basically two tempos. The *sorrow* song (e.g. "Steal Away") is performed in a slow, languorous manner, while the *jubilee* song (e.g. "Certainly, Lord") should be performed in a brisk walking tempo. Moderately slow gospel songs (e.g. "Praise Him") should never be performed sluggishly, but in the tempo of a *gospel* waltz, while the shout song (e.g. "I'm So Glad Jesus Lifted Me") should be performed at a fast tempo. Occasionally a congregation will elect the Baptist Lining Hymn style for a song, in which case the song should be performed without a pulse, instead assigning each syllable an amount of time equal to its importance in the text.

While most Negro Spirituals and gospel songs are sung in a tempo long associated with the song, the location of a song within the service may dictate a different tempo. If a jubilee song is used as a response to a prayer, the tempo may be much slower than that employed as an independent song, while a slow song may be given a faster tempo during such an activity as the "Peace." Regardless of the tempo assigned, maintain that tempo, always realizing that beneath the foreground tempo, there is a background tempo to which the singer must pay close attention to insure the lilt and forward motion required.

Improvisation

Altering, rearranging, and spontaneously composing a melodic line to a given harmony are some of the ways in which African Americans personalize music making, both vocally and instrumentally. The process can involve occasionally changing a single tone, substituting different tones for many of the prescribed tones, or completely paraphrasing a melody. In most cases this is not done as a result of knowing other tones of the chord, but by what sounds and feels "right." The experienced singer has a number of stock motives, fragments, or "runs" that can be used in almost any song, and in cases where this is not possible, the singer may simply repeat words or phrases for a number of times. Improvisation is not only applied to the melody, but rhythm, text, and harmony. Adding extra beats during rests, dividing pulses into two accents, or lengthening or shortening a note, adding to or subtracting from words in the original text, and interpolating passing and auxiliary chords to the original harmonies are all features of African American sacred singing.

Along with altering, rearranging, adding, and omitting tones in a given melody, there are timbre variations associated with the African American singing tradition. Among these are the bending of tones, slides, slurs, grunts, wails, runs, turns, chromaticisms, vocables (nonverbal outbursts), screams, and the use of falsetto. Since improvisation is spontaneous, often the singer has no knowledge of what will come forth. Despite this freedom, the singer must always strive to improvise in the style and in the context of the service. Above all, spontaneity is the ruling performance practice in all African American folk singing.

Instruments

While many of the songs in the hymnal might best be accompanied by organ or piano, others may be accompanied by a variety of instruments. There is no prescribed orchestration for gospel songs, but music directors are encouraged to be creative in assigning instruments for such songs. Since most gospel songs are improvised, they are open to accompaniment by any and all instruments. The basic instrument for gospel is the piano. Improvisation in gospel is relatively easy when it is understood that rhythm is much more important than tones. Unless the song is completely unfamiliar to a congregation, the keyboardist need not play the melody, but can provide an improvised accompaniment by dividing quarter notes into eighth notes, employing triplet figures, or play arpeggios. Since there are very few moments of silence in gospel, rests should be filled in with scales or scalar passages, runs, passing tones, turns, upper and lower neighbor tones, single note or octave interpolations, or glissandi. Balance and taste must dictate when and the amount of improvisation that can support a song. In general, if the singers are vocally active, the accompaniment should be subdued. Where there are open spaces in the singing, the keyboardists should fill in those sections. These devices may also be employed on organ. The Hammond organ, with Leslie B-3 speakers, has long been a favorite gospel music instrument. When organ and piano are used simultaneously, a decision regarding the leader and follower should be clearly understood.

The bass guitar is often used to accompany gospel. When a bass is used it should supply the root of the chord, with occasional uses of inversion, and should provide a strong accent on the primary beat of a rhythmic unit. The trap drummer should not only supply a strong primary and secondary beat, but the customary "back beat" as well. Horns may double the melody, but are much more effective playing riffs, countermelodies, descants or obbligatos, always being careful to play during the "response" and not the "call," which is assigned to the leader. Guitars may also double the melody but can be more effective strumming chords. Other percussion instruments, such as cymbals, tambourines, triangles, conga drums, bongos, and maracas are not intended to keep the beat, but are best used to provide variety within the rhythm. Gospel music bases its use of instruments on Psalm 150, where "everything that hath breath," including instruments, should be used to praise the Lord.

Body Rhythm

All African American folk sacred singing is accompanied by a rhythmic movement of the body. Not only does such movement provide greater rhythmic accentuation in the singing, but frees the body from tension and other "weights" that would interfere with worshipping. Handclapping, patting the feet, swaying, nodding the head, raising the arms upward, and shouting ("holy" dancing) are all common activities during traditional worship services. These activities should not be affected but should flow from the body as the singer releases unnecessary inhibitions and becomes more involved in the singing and worship.

African Americans firmly believe that the Lord is pleased when His children come before His presence with a song. For the greatest enjoyment of the songs in this hymnal, singers should follow the proclamation of the prophet: "lift up thy voice like a trumpet."

Horace Clarence Boyer, Ph.D.
General Editor

Service Music: Performance Notes

The service music section offers a diverse sampling of musical settings for use during the Holy Eucharist. Every effort has been made to include settings which embrace the African American musical tradition—spirituals, gospels, blues, jazz. We have also included some music indigenous to Africa, the Caribbean, and the broader Anglican Communion. Though this melange of musical expression offers many possibilities for creative worship, it is our fervent hope that priests, deacons, church musicians, and parish liturgical committees will select music for the eucharist which:

1. affords free expression;
2. promotes congregational participation and a sense of community;
3. captures the essence of the liturgy;
4. enhances spiritual growth and understanding; and
5. develops the parish's musical productivity and potential.

Because the "celebration" involves the entire congregation, the choir, though given some opportunity for individual expression, should maximize its chief function as the congregation's music leader. Therefore, service planners should choose settings that are within the congregation's grasp while occasionally encouraging the choir to introduce new or more difficult settings.

The editorial committee encourages within a single Eucharistic celebration the use of parts of the Mass from a variety of musical styles and genres. Such a practice, we believe, will serve to revitalize the service from Sunday to Sunday.

Following the settings of the *Gloria in Excelsis,* three alternate songs of praise appear which may be substituted freely for the standard *Gloria.* Likewise, additional musical responses follow the *Prayers of the People* and may be used before, during, or after the prayers from the *Book of Common Prayer* or prayers from other sources. In the *Book of Common Prayer,* that which is spoken may also be sung. To this end, we have also included settings for the "Memorial Acclamation," and the "Great Amen."

Psalms

The singing of the Psalms is a tradition born of the early Christian church which, in modern times, has been developed for practical application through Anglican and Simplified Anglican Chants. Of course, their performance in the more solemn and traditional "plainsong" is always an option. Care should be taken not to rush their performance but to govern their singing by the demands of natural flow and the rhythm of the words.

The refrains and Psalms at the end of the service music section are arranged for use at the Holy Eucharist. They may also be used at Morning and Evening Prayer, adding the *Gloria Patri* at the end of the Psalm, if desired (the *Gloria Patri* is omitted at the Eucharist). The Psalm texts and chants are only suggestions, for many of the refrains may be used with other Psalm texts, chants or tones, transposing where necessary. By varying the Psalm texts in this way, certain refrains may be used for several Sundays to foster congregational familiarity.

Simplified Anglican Chants

Simplified Anglican Chants are easily performed and mastered by the average congregation. Though written in four-part harmony, they should be performed in unison by the congregation; however, the choir may sing in parts. Each half verse of the Psalm is sung on the reciting note up to the last accented syllable. The word or syllable in bold print (last accented syllable) should be sung to the corresponding darkened whole note chord in the chant. When the Psalm text contains an odd number of verses, the second half of the chant is repeated for one of the verses.

We commend to you the riches of African American music—past and present—as we worshipfully challenge all to "make a joyful noise unto the Lord."

Carl Haywood, D.M.A.
Service Music Editor

The Editorial Committee

The Rt. Rev. Arthur B. Williams, Jr., Chair
Horace Clarence Boyer, General Editor
Carl Haywood, Service Music Editor
The Rev. Curtis W. Sisco, Liturgical Editor *(dec.)*
Doris P. Summey, Secretary

Deborah Harmon Hines
The Rev. Richard C. Martin
Robert L. Simpson
Irma Tillery

Staff

The Rev. Canon Harold T. Lewis
Marc S. Jones
Irene V. Jackson-Brown

Hymns and Songs

Lift Every Voice and Sing

1. Lift ev - 'ry voice and sing, Till earth and heav - en
2. Sto - ny the road we trod, Bit - ter the chast - 'ning
3. God of our wea - ry years, God of our si - lent

1. ring, Ring with the har - mo - nies of lib - er -
2. rod, Felt in the days when ___ hope un - born ___ had
3. tears, Thou who hast brought us ___ thus far on ___ the

1. ty; Let our re - joic - ing rise High as the list - 'ning ___
2. died; Yet with a stead - y beat, Have not our wear - y ___
3. way; Thou who hast by thy might, Led us in - to the ___

1. skies, Let it re - sound loud as the roll ___ ing sea. ___
2. feet Come to the place for which our fa - thers sighed? ___
3. light, Keep us for - ev - er in the path, ___ we pray. ___

1. Sing a song full of the faith that the dark past has taught us;
2. We have come o-ver a-way that with tears has been wa - tered;
3. Lest our feet stray from the pla-ces, our God, where we met thee;

1. Sing a song full of the hope that the pres-ent has
2. We have come, tread-ing our path through the blood of the
3. Lest our hearts, drunk with the wine of the world, we for

1. brought us; Fac - ing the ris - ing sun Of our new
2. slaugh - tered; Out from the gloom - y past, Till now we
3. get thee, Shad - owed be - neath Thy hand, May we for -

1. day be - gun, Let us march on till vic - to - ry is won.
2. stand at last Where the white gleam of our bright star is cast.
3. ev - er stand, True to our God, true to our na - tive land.

ADVENT

Behold Your God

Oh thou ___ that tell - est good ti - dings to Zi - on, Oh

thou ___ that tell - est good ti - dings to Je - ru - sa - lem:

Lift up your voice with strength, ___ Lift it up don't be a - fraid. Be -

hold ___ your ___ God. ___ A - - rise, ___ and shine, ___ for the

light of the world is come. Be - hold ___ your ___ God! ___

Words: Isaiah 40:9
Music: Kenneth W. Louis
Copyright © Kenneth W. Louis. Permission Requested.

Bye and Bye

O bye ___ and bye, ___ bye ___ and bye, I'm gon-na

lay down my heav-y ___ load. load.

1. I know my robe's gon-na fit me well, ___
2. O hell is deep and in dark des - pair, ___ I'm gon-na
3. O Chris - tian, can't you a - rise and tell, ___

lay down my heav-y ___ load.
1. I tried it on at the
2. So stop, po' sin - ner and
3. That Je - sus hath done

1. gates of hell. ___
2. don't go there. ___   I'm gon-na lay down my heav-y ___ load.
3. all things well. ___

Words: Traditional
Music: Negro Spiritual; arr. Edythe Ethelynn Woodruff (b.1970). Used by Permission.

Better Be Ready

Bet-ter be read - y; Bet-ter be read - y; Bet-ter be

Read - y; read - y

Bet-ter be read-y to try on your

read - y; Read-y to try your
try on your

read - y to try your

1. Bet-ter be

2. *Fine*

1. Oh!__ rise__ up chil - dren,__
2. What a glo - ri - ous morn - ing__
3. O__ shout_ you Christ - ians, you're
4. I __ soon_ shall reach that __

long white robe! long white robe _____ Hm _____

Words: Traditional
Music: Negro Spiritual; arr. R. Nathaniel Dett (1882 - 1943)

1. get your crown,
2. that will be,
3. gain-ing ground,
4. gold-en shore,

And by your Sav-ior's
Our friends and Je-sus
We'll shout old Sa-tan's
And sing the songs we

Bet-ter be read-y to try on your

Read-y to try your long white robe! Hm
try on your

to try your

1. side sit down.
2. we shall see.
3. king-dom down!
4. sang be-fore.

1.2.3.4. Bet-ter be

D.S.

Bet-ter be read-y to try on your

D.S.

Read-y to try your long white robe!
try on your

D.S.

To try your

Great Day 5

Great___ day! Great day, the righ-teous march-ing. Great___ day.___

Words: Traditional
Music: Negro Spiritual; harm. J. Jefferson Cleveland (1937-1988)
Harm. Copyright © 1981 Abingdon. Reprinted from *Songs of Zion* by permission.

Christ Is Coming

Christ _____ is com - ing: ___ Pre - pare the way. ___

Christ _____ is com - ing: ___ Pre - pare the way. ___

Fine

Christ is _____ com-ing. Christ is _____ com - ing.

D.C.

from *Advent Jazz Vespers II*
Music and Word adapt. by Edward V. Bonnemere
Copyright © Amity Music Corporation, 1475 Gaylord Terrace, Teaneck, New Jersey 07666.

I Want to Be Ready

1. John said that Je - ru - sa-lem was four-square,
2. When Pe-ter was preach-ing at Pen-te-cost,

1. I hope, good Lord, I'll meet you there,
2. O he was filled with the Ho-ly Ghost,

Words: Traditional
Music: Negro Spiritual; arr. R. Nathaniel Dett (1882-1943)
Arr. Copyright © 1936 Paul A. Schmitt Music Company. Copyright Assigned to Belwin Mills.
Made in U.S.A. International Copyright Secured. All Rights Reserved.
Used by permission of CPP/Belwin, Inc., P.O. Box 4340, Miami FL 33014.

Deep _____ ri - ver, my home is o - ver Jor - dan, _____

Deep _____ riv - er, Lord, I want to cross o - ver in - to

camp ground. Oh don't you want to go __ to that gos - pel __

feast, That prom - ised land __ where all __ is peace? Oh __

Deep _____ riv - er, Lord, I want to cross o - ver in - to camp ground.

Words: Traditional
Music: Negro Spiritual; arr. Carl Haywood (b. 1949), from *The Haywood Collection of Negro Spirituals,*
Copyright ©1992.

1. On __ Jor-dan's storm-y banks I stand, __ And cast a wish-ful eye;
2. All __ o'er those wide-ex-tend-ed plains,__ Shines one e-ter-nal day;
3. No __ chill-ing winds or poi-s'nous breath __ Can reach that health-ful shore;
4. When shall I reach that hap-py place __ And be for-ev-er blest?

%   Fine

1. To Ca-naan's fair and hap-py land, Where __ my pos - ses-sions lie.
2. There God the Son for-ev-er reigns, And __ scat-ters night a-way.
3. Sick-ness and sor-row, pain and death, Are __ felt and feared no more.
4. When shall I see my Fa-ther's face, And __ in God's bos-om rest?

D.S. Oh, who will come and go with me? I am bound for the prom-ised land.

D.S.

I am bound for the prom-ised land, _____ I am bound for the prom-ised land;

Words: Samuel Stennett (1727-1795)
Music: American Melody; adapt. Rigdon McCoy McIntosh (1836-1899); arr. Norman Johnson

10   **Oh! What a Beautiful City**

Oh! what a beau-ti-ful cit-y, Oh! what a

beau - ti - ful cit - y, Oh! what a beau - ti - ful cit - y,

Twelve gates - a to the cit - y, Hal - le - lu - jah!

1.
2. **Fine**

jah! 1. There's three gates in - a the East, _____ three gates _ in - a the
2. O, my Lord built - a that day, _____ that was _ just - a fore

1. West; _____ Three gates in - a the North, and three gates in - a the
2. square; _ wan-ted all - a you sin - ners to meet Him in - a the

D.C.

1. South, mak-ing it twelve gates - a to the cit - y, a - Hal - le - lu - jah.
2. air, 'cause He built twelve gates - a to the cit - y, a - Hal - le - lu - jah.

Words: Traditional
Music: Negro Spiritual; arr. Irma Tillery (b. 1925). Used by Permission.

Prepare Ye the Way of the Lord

Pre-pare ye the way ___ of the Lord. ___

Pre - pare ye the way ___ of the Lord. ___

Words: Isaiah 40:3-4, 9
Music: James E. Moore, Jr.

1.- 4.   *Final ending*   **Fine**

1. Make straight in the
2. Fill ev - 'ry
3. Go up to a
4. Say to all

1. des - ert _____ a high - way for our God.
2. val - ley, _____ bring all moun - tains low.
3. moun - tain _____ and shout with a loud voice.
4. peo - ple, _____ here _____ is your God.

D.S.

D.S.

We're Marching to Zion

1. Come, we that love the Lord, And let our joys be known; Join
2. Let those re-fuse to sing Who nev-er knew our God; But
3. The hill of Zi-on yields A thou-sand sa-cred sweets Be-
4. Then let our songs a-bound, And ev-'ry tear be dry; We're

1. in a song with sweet ac-cord, Join in a song with sweet ac-
2. chil-dren of the heav'n-ly King, But chil-dren of the heav'n-ly
3. fore we reach the heav'n-ly fields, Be-fore we reach the heav'n-ly
4. march-ing through Im-man-uel's ground, We're march-ing thro' Im-man-uel's

1. cord, And thus sur-round the throne, And thus sur-round the throne.
2. King, May speak their joys a-broad, May speak their joys a-broad.
3. fields, Or walk the gold-en streets, Or walk the gold-en streets.
4. ground, To fair-er worlds on high, To fair-er worlds on high.

We're march-ing to Zi-on, Beau-ti-ful, beau-ti-ful

We're march-ing on to Zi-on,

Zi - on; We're march - ing up-ward to Zi - on,

Zi - on, Zi - on,

The beau - ti - ful cit - y ___ of God. _____

Words: Isaac Watts (1674-1748)
Music: Robert S. Lowry (1826-1899)

My Lord, What a Morning 13

Harmony

My Lord, what a morn - ing, My Lord, what a morn - ing, ___ O

Fine

my Lord, what a morn - ing, When the stars be - gin to fall.

Hymn continues on the next page.

Words: Traditional
Music: Negro Spiritual

14

Soon and Very Soon

1. Soon and ver - y soon __ we are goin' to see the King, __
2. No more cry - in' there __ we are goin' to see the King, __
3. No more dy - in' there __ we are goin' to see the King, __
4. Soon and ver - y soon __ we are goin' to see the King; __

Words: Andrae Crouch (b. 1942)
Music: Andrae Crouch
Copyright © 1976 Bud John Songs, Inc./Crouch Music/ASCAP

1. Soon and ver - y soon __ we are goin' to see the King, __
2. No more cry - in' there __ we are goin' to see the King, __
3. No more dy - in' there __ we are goin' to see the King, __
4. Soon and ver - y soon __ we are goin' to see the King, __

1. Soon and ver - y soon __ we are goin' to see the King,
2. No more cry - in' there __ we are goin' to see the King,
3. No more dy - in' there __ we are goin' to see the King,
4. Soon and ver - y soon __ we are goin' to see the King,

__ Hal-le - lu - jah, Hal-le - lu - jah, __ we're goin' to see the King!

1. 2.   3. 4.

__ Hal - le - lu - jah, Hal - le - lu -

jah, Hal - le - lu - jah, Hal - le - lu - jah.

Climb-in'up d'moun - tain,__ chil - dren. Did-n't come here for to

Good Lawd, Ah

stay. If ah nev - er - more see you a-gain, ___ gon-na

Oh, my Lawd, __ and __

meet you at d' judg - ment day__

Hal - le - lu - jah, Lawd, Ah'm

Oh, Lawd,__   Oh, Lawd,__

1. He - brew chil-dren in de fier- y   fur-nace. And dey be-gin to pray,   And de
2. Dan - iel went__ in de li-on's den,__   And he be-gin to pray,   And de

Oh,   was-n't dat a might-y

1. good Lawd smote dat __ fi - yah out.
2. an - gel of de Lawd locked de li-on's jaw.

Words: Traditional
Music: Negro Spiritual; arr. Verolga Nix (b. 1933). Copyright © 1981 Abingdon.
Reprinted from *Songs of Zion* by permission.

day! Good Lawd, was-n't dat a might-y day! Dat's why Ah'm

You Are Near

16

Yah-weh, I know You are near, stand-ing al - ways at my side. You

Words: Psalm 139, Dan Schutte, SJ
Music: Dan Schutte, SJ; harm. Theophane Hytrek, OSF
Copyright © 1971, 1974, Daniel Schutte. Administered by New Dawn Music. All Rights Reserved.
Used by Permission.

guard me from the foe. And You lead me ___ in

Fine

ways e - ver - last - ing. _____

1. Lord, You have searched my heart, and You
2. Where can I run from Your love? If I
3. You know my heart and its ways, You who
4. Mar - vel - ous to me are Your works; how pro -

1. know when I sit and when I stand. Your _
2. climb to the heav - ens You are there; if I
3. formed me be - fore I was born, in the
4. found are Your thoughts, my Lord. E - ven

1. hand is up - on me pro - tect - ing me from death,
2. fly to the sun - rise or sail be - yond the sea,
3. se - cret of dark - ness be - fore I saw the sun
4. if I could count them, they num - ber as the stars,

D.C.

1. keep - ing me from harm. _____
2. still I'd find You there. _____
3. in my moth - er's womb. _____
4. You would still be there. _____

Rockin' Jerusalem

O Mar-y, O Mar-tha, O Mar-y, ring dem bells.

O Mar-y, O Mar-tha, O Mar-y, ring dem bells, I

hear arch-an-gels a rock-in' Je-ru-sa-lem, I hear arch-an-gels a

Fine

ring-in' dem bells. 1. Church get-tin' high-er!
2. New Je-ru-sa-lem! Rock-in' Je-ru-sa-lem!

D.C.

1. Church get-tin' high-er!
2. New Je-ru-sa-lem! ring-in' dem bells.

Words: Traditional
Music: Negro Spiritual; arr. Horace Clarence Boyer (b. 1935)
Arr. Copyright © 1992 Horace Clarence Boyer

Fine

D.C.

1. I looked o - ver Jor - dan, and what did I see ___
2. If you get ___ there be - fore ___ I do, ___
3. The bright - est day that ___ ev - er I saw ___
4. I'm some - times up and ___ some - times down, ___

1. Com-ing for to car - ry me home. A band ___ of an - gels
2. Com-ing for to car - ry me home. Tell all ___ my friends I'm
3. Com-ing for to car - ry me home. When Je - sus wash'd my
4. Com-ing for to car - ry me home. But still ___ my soul feels

1. com-ing af - ter me, ___ Com-ing for to car - ry me home. O,
2. com - ing too, ___ Com-ing for to car - ry me home. O,
3. sins a - way, ___ Com-ing for to car - ry me home. O,
4. heaven - ly bound, ___ Com-ing for to car - ry me home. O,

Swing low, sweet char - i - ot, ___ Com-ing for to car-ry me home.

Swing ___ low, sweet char - i - ot, ___ Com-ing for to car-ry me home.

Words: Traditional
Music: Negro Spiritual; arr. R. Nathaniel Dett (1882-1943)
Arr. Copyright © 1936 Paul A. Schmitt Music Company. Copyright assigned to Belwin Mills. Made in U.S.A.
International Copyright Secured. All Rights Reserved. Used by permission of CPP/Belwin, Inc., P.O. Box 4340,
Miami, FL 33014.

Wayfaring Stranger

1. I'm just a poor___ way-far-ing stran-ger,___ I'm trav'-ling through this world be-
2. I know dark clouds___ will gath-er o'er me,___ I know my path-way's rough and
3. I want to sing___ sal-va-tions sto-ry,___ In con-cert with ___ the blood-washed
4. I'll soon be free ___ from ev-ery tri-al, ___ This form will rest ___ be-neath the

1. low; ___ There is no sick-ness, toil, nor dan-ger, ___ In that bright
2. steep; ___ But gold-en fields ___ lie out be-fore me, ___ Where wea-ry
3. band; ___ I want to wear ___ a crown of glo-ry, ___ When I get
4. sod; ___ I'll drop the cross ___ of self-de-ni-al, ___ And en-ter

1. world ___ to which I go. ___ I'm go-ing there ___ to see my
2. eyes ___ no more shall weep. ___ I'm go-ing there ___ to see my
3. home ___ to that good land. ___ I'm go-ing there ___ to see my
4. in ___ my home with God. ___ I'm go-ing there ___ to see my

Words: Traditional
Music: American Folk Song; arr. Horace Clarence Boyer (b. 1935)
Arr. Copyright © 1992 Horace Clarence Boyer

1. fa - ther, __ I'm go - ing there____ no __ more to __ roam; ____
2. mo - ther, __ She said she'd meet____ me __ when I come; ____ I'm just a
3. bro - thers, __ They passed be - fore____ me __ one by one; ____
4. Sav - iour, __ Who shed for me____ His __ pre - cious blood; ____

go - ing o - ver Jor - dan, _ I'm just a go - ing o - ver home. __

When We All Get to Heaven

1. Sing the won-drous love of Je-sus, Sing His mer-cy and His grace;
2. While we walk the pil-grim path-way, Clouds will o-ver-spread the sky;
3. Let us then be true and faith-ful, Trust-ing, serv-ing ev-'ry day;
4. On-ward to the prize be-fore us! Soon His beau-ty we'll be-hold;

1. In the man-sion bright and bless-ed, He'll pre-pare for us a place.
2. But when trav-'ling days are o-ver, Not a shad-ow, not a sigh.
3. Just one glimpse of Him in glo-ry Will the toils of life re-pay;
4. Soon the pearl-y gates will o-pen; We shall tread the streets of gold.

When we all _____ get to heav-en, What a day of re-

When we all get to heav-en, What a

joic-ing that will be! _____ When we all _____ see

day of re-joic-ing that will be! When we all see

Je-sus, We'll sing and shout the vic-to-ry. _____

Je-sus, We'll sing and shout, and shout the vic-to-ry.

Words: Eliza Edmunds Hewitt (1851-1920)
Music: Emily Divine Wilson (1865-1942)

CHRISTMAS

Go, Tell It on the Mountain

Go, tell it on the moun - tain, o-ver the hills and ev- ery-where; go, tell it on the moun - tain, that Je - sus Christ _ is born.

1. While shep - herds kept their watch - ing o'er si - lent flocks by night,
2. The shep - herds feared and trem - bled, when lo! a - bove the earth,
3. Down in a low - ly man - ger the hum- ble Christ was born,

1. Be - hold through-out the heav - ens there shown a ho - ly light. ____
2. Rang out the an - gel cho - rus that hailed the Sav - ior's birth. ____
3. And God sent us sal - va - tion that bless - ed Christ - mas morn. ____

Words: Luke 2:8-20; adapt. John W. Work, Jr. (1871-1925)
Music: Negro Spiritual; adapt. and arr. William Farley Smith (b. 1941)
Words used by permission of Mrs. J. W. Work.
Adapt. and Arr. Copyright © 1989 *The United Methodist Hymnal* by permission.

Mary Borned a Baby

Words: Traditional
Music: Negro Spiritual; arr. Noah Francis Ryder (1914-1964)
Copyright © Noah Francis Ryder. Permission Requested.

Praise His name, praise His name.

Praise His name,

Jesus Came to Earth from Glory

1. Je - sus came to earth from glo - ry, That first Christ - mas morn.
2. As a child, the pure and low - ly Gave him great de - light.
3. Grown to man - hood, Pledged to du - ty, Je - sus taught and healed.

1. Shep - herds heard the an - gel sto - ry Christ was born.
2. Home and bread and toil were ho - ly In His sight.
3. From the li - lies in their beau - ty, Truths re - vealed.

Words: Hugh Sherlock (b. 1905)
Music: Doreen Potter
Copyright © 1981 Caribbean Conference of Churches

Rise Up, Shepherd, and Follow

Words: Traditional
Music: Negro Spiritual

That Boy-Child of Mary

That boy-child of Ma — ry was born in a sta — ble, a man-ger his
cra — dle in Beth - le - hem. _____

Fine

1. What shall we call   Him,
2. His name is Je - sus,
3. How can He save   us,
4. Gift of the Fa - ther,
5. One with the Fa - ther,
6. Glad - ly we praise Him,

D.C.

1. Child of the man - ger? What name is giv - en   in Beth-le - hem? __
2. God ev-er with   us,   God giv-en for   us   in Beth-le - hem? __
3. How can He help   us,   Born here a - mong us   in Beth-le - hem? __
4. To   hu-man moth - er, Makes Him our broth - er in Beth-le - hem? __
5. He is our Sav - ior, Heav - en-sent help - er in Beth-le - hem? __
6. Love and a - dore   Him, Give our-selves to   Him   in Beth-le - hem? __

Words: Luke 2:7; Tom Colvin (b. 1925)
Music: Traditional Malawi Melody; adapt. Tom Colvin (b. 1925)

Words: Joseph Mohr (1792-1848)
Music: Franz Gruber (1787-1863); arr. Horace Clarence Boyer (b. 1935)

1. _____ Sleep __ in heav - en - ly peace. _____
2. _____ Christ __ the Sav - ior is born. _____
3. _____ Je - sus, Lord, at thy birth. _____
4. _____ Rest __ in heav - en - ly peace. _____

Away in a Manger 27

1. A - way in a man-ger, no crib for a bed, The lit - tle Lord
2. The cat - tle are low-ing, the Ba - by a - wakes, But lit - tle Lord
3. Be near me, Lord Je - sus, I ask thee to stay Close by me for

1. Je - sus laid down His sweet head. The stars in the sky __ looked
2. Je - sus, no cry - ing He makes, I love thee, Lord Je - sus, Look
3. ev - er, and love me, I pray. Bless all the dear chil - dren in

1. down where He lay, The lit - tle Lord Je - sus a - sleep on the hay.
2. down from the sky, And stay by my cra - dle till morn-ing is nigh.
3. thy ten - der care, And fit us for heav - en to live with thee there.

Words: Anonymous
Music: James R. Murray (1841-1905); arr. Edythe Ethelynn Woodruff (b. 1970). Used by Permission.

LENT AND HOLY WEEK

Down at the Cross

1. Down at the cross where my Sav-ior died, Down where for cleans-ing from
2. I am so won-drous-ly saved from sin, Je - sus so sweet-ly a -
3. O, pre-cious foun - tain that saves from sin, I am so glad I have
4. Come to this foun - tain so rich and sweet; Cast your poor soul at the

1. sin I cried; There to my heart was the blood ap - plied;
2. bides with - in; There at the cross where He took me in;
3. en - tered in; There Je - sus saves me and keeps me clean;
4. Sav - ior's feet; Plunge in to - day, and be made com - plete;

Glo-ry to His name. Glo-ry to His name. __ Glo-ry to His name! __

There to my heart was the blood ap- plied; Glo - ry to His name.

Words: Elisha A. Hoffman (1839-1929)
Music: John H. Stockton (1813-1877)

1. Je - sus, keep me near the cross, There's a pre - cious foun - tain;
2. Near the cross, a trem - bling soul, Love and mer - cy found me;
3. Near the cross! O Lamb of God, Bring its scenes be - fore me;
4. Near the cross. I'll watch and wait, Hop - ing, trust - ing ev - er,

1. Free to all, a heal - ing stream Flows from Cal - v'ry's moun - tain.
2. There the Bright and Morn - ing Star Sheds its beams a - round me.
3. Help me walk from day to day With its shad - ows o'er me.
4. Till I reach the gold - en strand Just be - yond the riv - er.

In the cross, in the cross Be my glo - ry ev - er;

Till my rap - tured soul shall find Rest be - yond the riv - er.

Words: Fanny J. Crosby (1820-1915)
Music: William H. Doane (1832-1915)

1. A - las! and did my Sav - ior bleed, and
2. Was it for crimes that I have done, He
3. Well might the sun in dark - ness hide, and
4. Thus might I hide my blush - ing face while
5. But drops of tears can ne'er re - pay the

1. did my Sov' - reign die? Would He de - vote that
2. groaned up - on the tree? A - maz - ing pit - y!
3. shut its glo - ries in; when God, the might - y
4. His dear cross ap - pears; dis - solve my heart in
5. debt of love I owe; Here, Lord, I give my -

1. sa - cred head for sin - ners such as I?
2. Grace un-known! And love be - yond de - gree!
3. mak - er, died for His own crea - ture's sin.
4. thank - ful-ness, and melt mine eyes to tears.
5. self a - way; 'tis all that I can do.

At the cross, at the cross, where I first __ saw the light, and the

bur-den of my heart rolled a-way; it was there by faith I re-

Words: Isaac Watts, 1707; refrain Ralph E. Hudson, 1885
Music: Ralph E. Hudson, 1885

ceived my sight, and now I am hap-py all the day.

Lead Me to Calvary

1. King of my life I crown thee now, Thine shall the glo - ry be;
2. Show me the tomb where thou wast laid, Ten - der - ly mourned and wept;
3. Let me, like Ma - ry, through the gloom, Come with a gift to thee;
4. May I be will - ing, Lord, to bear Dai - ly my cross for thee;

1. Lest I for - get thy thorn - crowned brow, Lead me to Cal - va - ry.
2. An - gels in robes of light ar - rayed Guard - ed thee whilst Thou slept.
3. Show to me now the emp - ty tomb, - Lead me to Cal - va - ry.
4. E - ven thy cup of grief to share - Thou hast borne all for me.

Lest I for-get Geth - sem - a - ne, Lest I for-get thine ag - o - ny,

Lest I for-get thy love for me, Lead me to Cal - va - ry.

Words: Jennie Evelyn Hussey (1874-1958)
Music: William J. Kirkpatrick (1838-1921)

Calvary

Cal - va - ry, ___ Cal - va - ry, ___ Cal - va -

ry, ___ Cal - va - ry, ___ Cal - va - ry, ___

Fine

___ Cal - va - ry, ___ Sure - ly He died on ___ Cal - va - ry.

1. Ev - 'ry time I ___ think a - bout Je - sus, Ev - 'ry ___ time I ___
2. Don't you hear the ___ ham - mer ring - ing, Don't you ___ hear the ___

1. ___ think a - bout Je - sus, Ev - ry time I ___ think a - bout Je - sus,
2. ___ ham - mer ring - ing, Don't you hear the ___ ham - mer ring - ing,

Words: Traditional
Music: Negro Spiritual; arr. Carl Haywood (b. 1949), from *The Haywood Collection of Negro Spirituals*,
Copyright © 1992.

Sure - ly He died on ____ Cal - va - ry.

3. Don't you hear Him calling His Father? Surely He died on Calvary.
4. Don't you hear Him say, "It is finished." Surely He died on Calvary.
5. Jesus furnished my salvation. Surely He died on Calvary.
6. Sinner do you love my Jesus? Surely He died on Calvary.

He Never Said a Mumbalin' Word   33

1. They cru - ci - fied my Lord, ____ and He nev - er said a mum-ba-lin'
2. They nailed Him to a tree, ____ and He nev - er said a mum-ba-lin'

1. word; They cru - ci - fied my Lord, ____ and He nev - er said a mum-ba-lin'
2. word; They nailed Him to a tree, ____ and He nev - er said a mum-ba-lin'

1. word. Not a word, ____ not a word, ____ not a word.
2. word. Not a word, ____ not a word, ____ not a word.

3. They pierced Him in the side.
4. The blood came streamin' down.
5. He hung His head and died.

Words: Traditional
Music: Negro Spiritual; arr. Carl Haywood (b. 1949), from *The Haywood Collection of Negro Spirituals*,
Copyright © 1992.

He Will Remember Me

1. When on the cross of Cal-v'ry The Lord was cru-ci-fied;
2. O what a shame to kill Him There on that rug-ged cross;
3. At His dear feet I'm kneel-ing. My sins I now con-fess;

1. The mob stood 'round a-bout Him And mocked un-til He died.
2. But such a death was need-ed To res-cue all the lost.
3. I bow in deep re-pent-ance, My soul He'll sure-ly bless.

1. Two thieves were nailed be-side Him To share the ag-o-ny,
2. His blood was made a ran-som To set the cap-tives free,
3. My blind-ed eyes He o-pens So that the light I see,

1. But one of them cried out to Him, "O Lord, re-mem-ber me."
2. I know that I'm in-clud-ed, and He will re-mem-ber me.
3. And when I reach the pearl-y gates, He will re-mem-ber me.

Words: E. M. Bartlett (1885-1941)
Music: E. M. Bartlett
Copyright © 1976 Albert E. Brumley & Sons/SESAC. All Rights Reserved.
Used by permission of Integrated Copyright Group, Inc.

O How He Loves You and Me

1. O how He loves you and me.
2. Je - sus to Cal - vary did go,

1. O how He loves you and me;
2. His love for the worlds to show;

1. He gave His life, what more could He give;
2. What He did there brought hope from de - spair;

1. O how He loves you, O how He loves me,
2. O how He loves you, O how He loves me,

1. O how He loves you and me.
2. O how He loves you and me.

Words: Kurt Kaiser (b. 1934)
Music: Kurt Kaiser

O Sacred Head, Sore Wounded

Words: Paulus Gerhard (1607-1676)
Music: David Hurd (b. 1950)

1. round - ed _____ with mock - ing _____
2. pir - ed, _____ and quenched the _____
3. va - tion _____ up - on the _____
4. sor - row, _____ thy pit - y _____
5. quail not _____ in death's most _____

1. crown of _ thorn; what _____
2. light of _ light. Ah _____
3. cross to _ die. Ah, _____
4. with - out _ end? Oh, _____
5. fear - ful _ hour; that _____

1. sor - row mars thy _____ grand - eur? Can _____
2. me! for whom thou _____ di - est, hide _____
3. keep my heart thus _____ mov - ed to _____
4. make me thine for - ev - er! and _____
5. I may fight be - friend - ed, and _____

1. death thy___ bloom de - flower?
2. not so___ far thy grace,
3. stand thy___ cross be - neath,
4. should I___ faint - ing ___ be,
5. see in___ my last ___ strife

1. O ___ coun - ten - ance whose splen - dor
2. show ___ me, O Love most high - est,
3. to ___ mourn thee, well - be - lov - ed,
4. Lord, ___ let me nev - er, nev - er,
5. to ___ me thine arms ex - tend - ed

1. the hosts of ___ heav'n a - dore!
2. the bright - ness ___ of thy _ face.
3. yet thank thee ___ for thy _ death.
4. out - live my ___ love for _ thee.
5. up - on the ___ cross of _ life.

Were You There?

1. Were you there when they cru-ci-fied my Lord? _____ Were you
2. Were you there when they nailed Him to the tree? _____ Were you
3. Were you there when they laid Him in the tomb? _____ Were you
4. Were you there when He rose up from the grave? _____ Were you

1. there when they cru-ci-fied my Lord?
2. there when they nailed Him to the tree?
3. there when they laid Him in the tomb?
4. there when He rose up from the grave?

O! _____

Some-times it caus-es me to trem-ble, trem-ble, trem-ble.

1. Were you there when they cru-ci-fied my Lord? _____
2. Were you there when they nailed Him to the tree? _____
3. Were you there when they laid Him in the tomb? _____
4. Were you there when He rose up from the grave? _____

Words: Traditional
Music: Negro Spiritual; arr. Charles Winfred Douglas (1867-1944)

The Old Rugged Cross

1. On a hill far a - way stood an old rug-ged cross,
2. Oh, that old rug-ged cross so de-spised by the world,
3. In the old rug-ged cross, stained with blood so di - vine,
4. To the old rug-ged cross I will ev - er be true,

1. The___ em - blem of suf - f'ring ___ and shame; _____
2. Has a won - drous at - trac - tion for me; _____
3. A___ won - drous beau - ty I see; _____
4. Its___ shame and re - proach glad - ly bear; _____

1. And I love that old cross where the dear - est and best
2. For the dear Lamb of God left His glo - ry a - bove,
3. For 'twas on that old cross Je - sus suf - fered and died,
4. Then He'll call me some day to my home far a - way,

1. For a world of lost sin - ners was slain. _____
2. To___ bear it to dark Cal - va - ry. _____
3. To___ par - don and sanc - ti - fy me. _____
4. Where His glo - ry for - ev - er I'll share. _____

Words: George Bennard (1873-1960)
Music: George Bennard

Hymn continues on the next page.

old rug - ged cross _____

So I'll cher - ish the cross, the old rug - ged cross,

Till my tro - phies at last I lay down; _____

old rug - ged cross, _____

I will cling to the cross,__ the old rug - ged cross,

And ex - change it some day for a crown. _____

39

There Is a Fountain

1. There__ is a foun - tain filled with blood Drawn__
2. The___ dy - ing thief re - joiced to see That ___
3. Thou__ dy - ing Lamb, Thy pre - cious blood Shall __
4. E'er__ since by faith I saw the stream Thy__
5. Then__ in a no - bler, sweet - er song, I'll__

1. from Im - man - uel's veins; And___ sin - ners, plunged be
2. foun - tain in___ his day; And___ there may I, though
3. nev - er lose___ its pow'r; Till___ all the ran - somed
4. flow - ing wounds___ sup - ply; Re - deem - ing love has
5. sing Thy pow'r___ to save; When___ this poor, lisp - ing

1. neath that flood, Lose___ all their guilt - y stains:___ Lose___
2. vile as he, Wash___ all my sins a - way:___ Wash___
3. Church of God Are___ saved, to sin no more:___ Are___
4. been my theme, And___ shall be till I die: ___ And___
5. stamm - 'ring tongue Lies___ si - lent in the grave:___ Lies___

1. all their guilt - y stains, ___ Lose all their guilt - y___ stains; And___
2. all my sins a - way, ___ Wash all my sins___ a - way; And___
3. saved, to sin no more, ___ Are saved, to sin no___ more; Till___
4. shall be till I die, ___ And shall be till___ I___ die, Re -
5. si - lent in the grave, ___ Lies si - lent in___ the___ grave; When___

1. sin - ners, plunged be - neath that flood, Lose___ all their guilt - y stains.
2. there may I, though vile as he, Wash___ all my sins a - way
3. all the ran - somed Church of God Are___ saved, to sin no more.
4. deem - ing love has been my theme, And___ shall be till I die.
5. this poor lisp - ing, stamm - 'ring tongue Lies___ si - lent in the grave.

Words: William Cowper (1731-1800)
Music: American Melody; arr. Lowell Mason (1792-1872)

He 'Rose

1. They cru - ci - fied my Sav - ior and
2. Then Jo - seph begged his bod - y and
3. Sis - ter Ma - ry, she came run - ning, a -
4. An an - gel came from heav - en and

1. nailed him to the tree, they cru - ci - fied my
2. laid it in the tomb, then Jo - seph begged his
3. look - ing for my Lord, Sis -ter Ma - ry, she came
4. rolled the stone a - way, an an - gel came from

1. Sav - ior and nailed him to the tree, they
2. bod - y and laid it in the tomb, then
3. run - ning, a - look - ing for my Lord, Sis - ter
4. heav - en and rolled the stone a - way, an

1. cru - ci - fied my Sav - ior and nailed him to the tree, ___ And the
2. Jo - seph begged his bod - y and laid it in the tomb, ___ And the
3. Ma - ry, she came run - ning, a - look - ing for my Lord, ___ And the
4. an - gel came from heav - en and rolled the stone a - way, ___ And the

Words: Traditional
Music: Negro Spiritual; arr. William Farley Smith (b. 1941)
Arr. Copyright © 1989 The United Methodist Publishing House.
Reprinted from *The United Methodist Hymnal* by permission.

Lord will bear my spir - it home.

He 'rose, He 'rose, He 'rose _ from the dead! He
He 'rose He 'rose

'rose, He 'rose, He 'rose _ from the dead! He
He 'rose He 'rose

'rose, He 'rose, He 'rose _ from the dead, _ and the
He 'rose He 'rose

Lord will bear _____ my spir - it home.

Christ Has Arisen

Christ has a - ris - en, Al - le - lu - ia. Re - joice and praise Him, Al - le - lu - ia. For our Re - deem - er burst from the tomb, E - ven from death dis - pel - ling its gloom. Let us sing praise to Him with end - less joy. Death's fear - ful sting He has come to de - stroy, Our sin for giv - ing, Al - le - lu - ia. Je - sus is liv - ing, Al - le - lu - ia.

Words: Swahili Text; tr. Howard Olson
Music: Haya Tune; *Tumshandilie Mungu*, Makumira, Tanzania; harm. Carl Haywood (b. 1949), from *Songs of Praise*, Harm. Copyright © 1992. Words and Music Reprinted from *Lead Us Lord* by Howard S. Olson, Copyright © 1974 Augsburg Publishing House. Used by permission of Augsburg Fortress.

1. I serve a ris-en Sav-ior, He's in the world to-day;
2. In all the world a-round me I see His lov-ing care,
3. Re-joice, re-joice. O Chris-tian, lift up your voice and sing.

1. I know that He is liv-ing, what-ev-er oth-ers say;
2. And though my heart grows wea-ry I nev-er will de-spair;
3. E-ter-nal hal-le-lu-jahs to Je-sus Christ, the King!

1. I see His hand of mer-cy, I hear His voice of cheer,
2. I know that He is lead-ing through all the storm-y blast,
3. The hope of all who seek Him, the help of all who find,

1. And just the time I need Him He's al-ways near.
2. The day of His ap-pear-ing will come at last.
3. None oth-er is so lov-ing, so good and kind.

Words: Alfred H. Ackley (1887-1960)
Music: Alfred H. Ackley

He lives, ___ He lives, ___ Christ Je - sus lives ___ to - day! ___

He lives, He lives,

He walks with me and talks with me a - long life's nar - row way. ___

He lives, ___ He lives, ___ sal - va - tion to im - part! ___

He lives, He lives,

You ask me how I know He lives? He lives with-in my heart. ___

43

Because He Lives

1. God sent His Son, ___ they called Him Je - sus; ___ He came to love, ___
2. How sweet to hold ___ a new-born ba - by, ___ And feel the pride, ___
3. And then one day ___ I'll cross the riv - er; ___ I'll fight life's fi -

1. ___ heal, and for - give; _____ He lived and died _____ to buy my
2. ___ and joy he gives; _____ But great- er still _____ the calm as-
3. - nal war with pain; _____ And then as death _____ gives way to

1. par- don, _____ An emp-ty grave is there to prove my Sav-ior lives. _____
2. sur- rance, _____ This child can face un- cer-tain days be-cause He lives. _____
3. vic- t'ry, _____ I'll see the lights of glo- ry and I'll know He lives. _____

Be-cause He lives _____ I can face to- mo- row; _____ Be-cause He lives _____

___ all fear is gone; _____ Be- cause I know _____ He holds the

fu - ture, _____ And life is worth the liv-ing just be-cause He lives. _____

Words: Gloria Gaither (b. 1942) and William Gaither (b. 1936)
Music: William Gaither (b. 1936)

BLACK SAINTS

Blessed Absalom

(February 13)

1. Born in bond-age, born in shack-les, Born stripped of all dig-ni-ty,
2. Seek-ing to ex-pand hor-i-zons, Bi-ble, pri-mer he did find;
3. When in Phi-la-del-phia set-tled, He sought per-sons in great need,
4. One fine morn-ing, while at wor-ship, Wrested from his knees in pray-er;

1. Abs'-lom Jones was bound, de-ter-mined, That he would one day be free.
2. To each word he was at-ten-tive, Learn-ing, lest he fall be-hind.
3. Ded-i-ca-ted to em-pow'r-ment, His own peo-ple did he lead.
4. He, his friends, were thus e-vic-ted: "You no more may praise God here."

1. Bless-ed Abs'-lom, leads us, guides us, In the bonds of u-ni-ty.
2. Bless-ed Abs'-lom, lib-er-ates us From the pri-son of our mind.
3. Bless-ed Abs'-lom, pray that we from All in-diff'-rence may be freed.
4. Bless-ed Abs'-lom, pray that we may Stand stead-fast and per-se-vere.

5. Founded he Saint Thomas' Church for
Afric's sons and daughters blest;
Full-fledged members of Christ's Body,
They no longer were oppressed.
Blessed Abs'lom, pray that we may
Be the church at Christ's behest.

6. Blessed Abs'lom Jones, first priest of
Afric's stock within our fold;
May we, inspired by your witness
Raise up priests with hearts of gold!
Blessed Abs'lom, pioneer, prophet
May your story long be told!

7. Praise to Christ the Liberator;
Praise Creator ever blest;
Praise the Spirit, Source of comfort
North to south, and east to west:
Blessed Abs'lom, priest, exemplar,
In God's bosom now at rest.

Words: Harold T. Lewis (b. 1947)
Music: *Lauda Anima*, John Goss (1800-1880)
Words Copyright © 1992 Harold T. Lewis

(August 28 or May 5)

1. O Mon-i-ca, blest mo-ther, A well of ho-ly tears; For thy dear son, Au-gus-tine, You shed for ma-ny years. That he might learn the faith that the Lord's A-pos-tles taught, But far from Af-ric's coast, strange Phi-los-o-phies he sought.

2. But Je-sus, Word In-car-nate Re-vealed to him the Truth; Aug-us-tine, thus con-vert-ed, For-sook his way-ward youth. Re-nounc-ing Sa-tan's cun-ning, Pre-vailed he in that hour; And at the hands of Am-brose Re-ceived bap-ti-sm's pow'r.

3. Re-turned to his own home-land, As-sumed he Hip-po's see; Staunch cham-pion of the faith, He fought each her-e-sy. He taught the Church is ho-ly, Though sin-ners do a-bound; That in gifts sa-cra-ment-al Is true grace to be found.

4. Aug-us-tine, faith-ful bi-shop, Con-fes-sor to the end, In-flame our hearts with pas-sion For Je-sus, Lord and Friend. Au-gus-tine, ho-ly doc-tor, Thou son of Af-ric's sod, Help us to reach the gates of The Ci-ty of our God.

Words: Harold T. Lewis (b. 1947), Copyright © 1992.
Music: Marvin Curtis (b. 1951), Copyright © 1991

Blessed Martin, Pastor, Prophet

(January 15 or April 4)

1. Ho - ly God, you raise up proph - ets; Praise and hon - or do we sing,
2. Mo - ral con - science of his na - tion, Re - con - cil - ing black and white,
3. Teach - er of Christ - like non - vio - lence To the out - cast, poor and meek;
4. Preach - er of Christ's love for neigh - bor, He won No - bel's prize for peace;

1. For your faith - ful, hum - ble ser - vant, Doc - tor Mar - tin Luth - er King.
2. Dreamed he of a just so - cie - ty, we must car - ry on his fight.
3. Great - er weap - on 'gainst op - pres - sion Is to turn the o - ther cheek.
4. Peo - ples, beat your swords to plough - shares, Wars 'twixt na - tions all shall cease.

Refrain

Bless - ed Mar - tin, pas - tor, proph - et, you the moun - tain - top did see;

Bless - ed Mar - tin, ho - ly mar - tyr: Pray that we may _ all be free.

5. Champion of oppressed humanity
   Suff'ring throughout all the world;
   He offered pride and dignity
   Let Christ's banner be unfurled!
   Refrain

6. So, when felled by sniper's bullet,
   Under heavens overcast,
   He could cry, "Thank God Almighty,
   I am free, I'm free at last!"
   Refrain

Words: Harold T. Lewis (b. 1947), Copyright © 1992
Music: *Martin's Song* by Carl Haywood (b. 1949), from *Songs of Praise*, Copyright © 1992

(September 13)

1. O Cyprian, convert to the faith, Made bishop of the Carthage See, Beset, by schism, war and strife, Preached to the faithful unity.
2. O Cyprian, you did teach that we who God Almighty Father call, Must claim the church, The Bride of Christ As the true mother of us all.
3. O Cyprian, you did teach that we outside the church cannot be saved, Help us to bring forth penitents Unto Christ's font, that they be laved.
4. Steadfast defender of the truth, through Afric's coast you gained renown, Who persecuted, and besieged, Received, at last, the martyr's crown.

5. O Cyprian bishop, martyr blest
   Pray for us at God's heav'nly throne,
   That we, who Christ's true faith confess
   May Father, Son and Spirit own.

Words: Harold T. Lewis (b. 1947)
Music: *Rockingham*, from Second Supplement to Psalmody in Miniature, c. 1780; harm. Edward Miller (1731-1807)

Blessed Monica

(May 4)

1. In Af - ric's north - ern coast - land When Moth - er Church was young,
2. Ex - em - plar for all moth - ers, And pat - ron saint of wives,
3. Saint Mo - ni - ca en - treat - ed The throne of heav'n - ly grace,
4. In Os - tia's port, Au - gus - tine Heard her last dy - ing word;

1. Was born the ho - ly wo - man Of whom this hymn is sung.
2. She led her spouse and child - ren In ho - ly, Christ - ian lives.
3. That her dear son, Au - gus - tine The Gos - pel might em - brace.
4. He wished his moth - er's bo - dy In Af - ric's soil in - terred.

1. O Mon - i - ca, be - lov - ed be - fore God thee we own, ___
2. Af - fec - tion, pa - tience, wis - dom, True zeal and con - stan - cy: ___
3. Her tear - ful prayers were an - swered, Her heart no long - er ri - ven;
4. "No place is far from God," ___ Was her most ur - gent plea; ___

1. Our con - stant in - ter - ces - sor Be - fore His heav'n - ly throne.
2. With these gifts God en - dowed her And ho - ly Char - i - ty.
3. Con - fes - sor, bish - op, doc - tor She to the Church has giv'n.
4. "When at God's ho - ly al - tar Do there re - mem - ber me."

5. O Saint of perserverance   To whom we raise our praises
    Be with us as we pray;   As will be ever meet,
    That we with zeal and ardor   To Father, Son Eternal
    Might serve our God alway: And Holy Paraclete.

Words: Harold T. Lewis (b. 1947)
Music: *Lancashire*, Henry Thomas Smart (1813-1879)

Simon of Cyrene

(May 12) also suitable for Passiontide

1. O Je - sus scourged, de - rid - ed, mocked, up-
2. The sol - diers spat u - pon His face, His
3. His strength gave out, He tried in vain, Gol-
4. He came up from Cy - re - ne When the

1. Cal - va-ry's hill did tread; But un - der - load of
2. rai - ment did they strip; And thus ex - posed to
3. go - tha to as - cend; And so it was that
4. sol - diers him did seize; He was com - pelled to

1. splin - t'ry wood He fell u - pon His head.
2. com - mon gaze He suf - fered 'neath the whip.
3. Si - mon blest Be - came our Lord's dear friend.
4. bear the cross and so Je - sus did please.

5. His muscular frame bore Christ's own Tree
   Along the Sacred Way;
   "O Jesus, who will die for me
   I'll follow Thee alway."

6. O Simon, joyful crucifer
   Before the throne of grace:
   Pray that we who shall bear His cross
   May see Him face to face.

The melody may be sung in canon at distances of either two or three beats.

Words: Harold T. Lewis (b. 1947), Copyright © 1992.
Music: *New Britain*, from *Virginia Harmony*, 1831; adapt. Edwin Othello Excell (1851-1921);
harm. Austin Cole Lovelace (b. 1919), Harm. Copyright © 1964 Abingdon Press

Philip the Evangelist

(October 11)

1. The an-gel said to __ Phil - ip: "Go to a des - ert place."
2. The E - thi-ope re - spond - ed: "Lead me and be my guide."
3. They trav-elled in the __ char - iot, And came up - on a brook;
4. Saint Phil - lip told the __ E - thiope: "Be - lieve with all your heart;

1. And there he found an __ E - thiope, the treas - urer __ to __ Can - dace,
2. Ex - plain the scrip-ture __ to me; "Here, sit down __ at __ my side."
3. The E - thi - ope, ex - ci - ted then looked up __ from his book.
4. And God the Ho - ly __ Spir - it Will His own __ gift im - part."

1. Who sat with - in his char - iot with Ho - ly Writ in hand.
2. Then Phil- ip ex - e - ge - ted I - sai - ah's Ho - ly word.
3. "See Phil- ip, here is wa - ter," He said, and stopped his steed!
4. "I do be - lieve that Je - sus Is God's true, on - ly son."

Words: Harold T. Lewis (b. 1947), Copyright © 1992.
Music: *Nyland,* Finnish Folk Melody; adapt. David Evans (1874-1948)
Copyright © from *The Revised Church Hymnary 1927* by permission of Oxford University Press.

1. Asked Phil - ip: "Can you,_ bro - ther, the Pro - phet un - der - stand?"
2. And preached un - to the _ E - thiope that Je - sus Christ is Lord.
3. "What can now," he im - plored him, "My bap - tism ___ im - pede?"
4. And with these words, the _ treas - urer A great - er_ treas - ure won.

5. O Philip, the evangelist
   You brought to Afric's seed
 The Gospel of our Savior
   In thought, and word and deed,

O may we share Thy fervor
   And press on towards the prize;
And heed our Lord's commission
   To teach, preach and baptize.

Salamu Maria

(March 25 or August 15)

51

1. Sa - la - mu Ma - ri - a,   ee   ma - ma,   Sa - la - mu, sa -
   (Hail   Mar - y,   Oh   moth - er,   Hail,   hail
2. U - me - ja - a nee - ma, ee   ma - ma.
   (Full   of   grace   oh   moth - er,

la - mu Ma - ri - a,   Ma - ri - a;   ri - a.
Mar - y,   Mar - y;   y.)*

Words: African Folk Hymn
Music: African Melody

PRAISE TO GOD

God Has Smiled on Me

God has smiled on me, __ He has set __ me free. __

God has smiled on me, __ He's been good __ to me. __

1. He is ____ the source ____ of all ____
2. A light ____ un - to ____ my path ____

1. ____ my joy, He fills ____ me with ____ His love ____ The grace
2. ____ is He, my strength ____ when I ____ would fall ____ He guides

1. ____ that I ____ em - ploy, ____ He sends: down from ____ a - bove. ____
2. ____ each day ____ for me, ____ God is my all ____ and all. ____

D.C.

Glo-ry to God in the high-est, He is the might-y King, Mas-ter of ever-y thing, The cap-tain of my soul, The u-ni-verse con-trol, God is the one true ex-pres-sion of life. He's the cre-a-tor, A great cre-a-tor, Hea-ven and earth His great-ness pro-claim. The cap-tain of my soul, The u-ni verse con-trol,

Words: Turner Hughes
Music: Frank E. White

Ho - nor and ma - jes - ty se - cond to none.____

Nearer, My God, to Thee 54

1. Near - er, my God, to Thee, Near - er to Thee!
2. Though like the wan - der - er, The sun goes down,
3. There let the way ap - pear, Steps un - to heav'n;
4. Then, with my wak - ing thoughts, Bright with Thy praise,
5. Or if on joy - ful wing, Cleav - ing the sky,

1. E'en though it be a cross That ___ rais - eth me;
2. Dark - ness be o - ver me, My ___ rest a stone;
3. All that Thou send - est me, In ___ mer - cy giv'n;
4. Out of my ston - y griefs, Beth - el I'll raise;
5. Sun, moon and stars for - got, Up - wards I fly,

1. Still all my song would be
2. Yet in my dreams I'd be
3. An - gels to beck - on me Near - er, my God, to Thee,
4. So by my woes to be
5. Still all my song shall be

Near - er my God, to Thee, Near - er to Thee.

Words: Sarah F. Adams (1805-1848)
Music: Bethany, Lowell Mason (1792-1872)

In God We Trust

1. In God we trust, with all our
(2. In) God we trust, wher - ev - er

God we trust

1. heart and soul, In God we trust to
2. we may roam, In God we trust to

1. reach our righ - teous goal, En - shrined in
2. bless our land and home, Through all our

1. Thee for - ev - er may we be, Come what
2. days we'll al - ways sing His praise, Come what

1. may, Keep faith and pray, in God we trust, in
2. may, Our hearts will pray, in God we trust, in

God we trust,

Words: Anonymous
Music: Anonymous; arr. C. Julian Parrish (b. 1911)
Folks year round worship song, arranged for use in hymnals and supplements to hymnals by C. Julian Parrish.

1. God _____ we trust, _____ In
2. God _____ we trust. _____

Praise God from Whom All Blessings Flow

56

Praise God from whom all ___ bless - ings flow,

Praise Him all cre - tures here be - low.

Praise Him a - bove ye ___ heav - en - ly host.

Praise Fa - ther, Son and Ho - ly Ghost.

Words: Isaac Watts (1675-1748); and William Keathe (d. 1593); adapt. Thomas Ken (1637-1711)
Music: John Hatton (d. 1793); adapt. George Coles; harm. Roberta Martin (1912-1969)

Oh Lord, How Perfect Is

1. Oh Lord, How per-fect is _ your name. _____ In
2. When I be - hold _ thy_ heav'ns grand The

1. earth ___ great thy fame, A - bove the hea - vens thou didst ___
2. stars at thy com - mand Lord, What is man that thou shouldst_

1. set Thy glo- ry gra-cious Lord, and yet out of the mouths of babes calls _
2. heed his call or vi-sit his seed, Near_ an-gels then have fixed _ stead -

Words: Hymn Tune
Music: Irma Tillery (b. 1925). Used by Permission.

1. Thee, Thy strength to ___ still the __ en - e - my!
2. fast the ho - nor __ and glo-ry crown His head.

The Lord Is My Light

58

The Lord is my light and my sal - va - tion, the Lord is my

light and my sal - va - tion, the Lord is my light and

my sal - va - tion; whom shall I ____ fear?

Hymn continues on the next page.

Words: Lillian Bouknight
Music: Lillian Bouknight; arr. Paul Gainer
Copyright © 1980 Savgos Music, Inc. International Copyright Secured. All Rights Reserved. Used by Permission.

My Heavenly Father Watches Over Me

1. I trust in God wher-ev-er I may be, _____ Up - on the
2. He makes the rose an ob-ject of His care, _____ He guides the
3. I trust in God, for, in the li - on's den, _____ On bat - tle -
4. The val - ley may be dark, the sha-dows deep, _____ But oh, the

1. land _____ or on the roll - ing sea; _____ For come what
2. ea - gle through the path-less air; _____ And sure - ly
3. field, _____ or in the pris - on pen; _____ Through praise or
4. shep - herd guards His lone - ly sheep; _____ And through the

1. may, _____ from day to day, _____
2. He _____ re - mem-bers me, _____ My heav'n-ly Fa-ther watch-es o - ver
3. blame, _____ through flood or flame, _____
4. gloom, _____ He'll lead me home, _____

me. _____ I trust in God, _____ I know He cares for me, On moun-tain

Hymn continues on the next page.

Words: W. C. Martin
Music: Charles H. Gabriel (1856-1932); arr. J. Jefferson Cleveland (1937-1988) and Verolga Nix (b. 1933)

bleak or on the storm-y sea;___ Though bil-lows roll,_____ He keeps my

soul,_____ My heav'n-ly Fa-ther watch-es o - ver me._____

1. O Lord my God, when I in awe-some won - der Con - sid - er
2. When through the woods and for-est glades I wan - der And hear the
3. And when I think that God, his Son not spar - ing, Sent him to
4. When Christ shall come with shout of ac - cla - ma - tion And take me

1. all the worlds* thy hands have made,___ I see the stars I hear the roll - ing*
2. birds sing sweet - ly in the trees,___ When I look down from loft - y moun - tain
3. die, I scarce can take it in, ___ That on the cross, my bur - den glad - ly
4. home, what joy shall fill my heart!___ Then I shall bow in hum - ble ad - or -

*The translator's original words are "works" and "mighty."

Words: Stuart K. Hine (1899-1989)
Music: Swedish Folk Melody; arr. Stuart K. Hine
Words and arr. © 1953. Renewed 1981 MANNA MUSIC, INC. P.O. Box 218, Pacific City, OR 97135.
International Copyright Secured. All Rights Reserved. Used by Permission.

1. thun - der,   Thy pow'r through-out   the u - ni - verse dis - played. _____
2. gran- deur,   And hear   the brook   and feel the gen - tle breeze. _____
3. bear - ing,   He bled and died   to take a - way my sin. _____
4. ra - tion,   And there pro - claim,   my God, how great thou art. _____

Then sings my soul,   my Sav - ior, God, to Thee; _____ How great Thou

art, _____ how great Thou art! _____ Then sings my soul,   my Sav - ior God, to

Thee: _____ How great Thou art, _____ how great Thou art! _____

The Right Hand of God

1. The right hand of God is writ-ing in our land,
2. The right hand of God is point-ing in our land,
3. The right hand of God is strik-ing in our land,
4. The right hand of God is heal-ing in our land,
5. The right hand of God is plant-ing in our land,

1. Writ - ing with pow - er and with love,
2. Point - ing the way we must go.
3. Strik-ing out at en - vy, hate, and greed.
4. Heal-ing bro - ken bod - ies, minds, and souls.
5. Plant-ing seeds of free - dom, hope, and love.

1. Our con - flicts and our fears, our tri-umphs and our
2. So cloud-ed is the way, so eas - i - ly we
3. Our sel - fish - ness and lust, our pride and deeds un -
4. So won-drous is its touch with love that means so
5. In these Ca - rib - bean lands, let His peo- ple all join

1. tears Are re - cord-ed by the right hand of God.
2. stray, But we're guid-ed by the right hand of God.
3. just Are de - stroyed by the right hand of God.
4. much, When we're healed by the right hand of God.
5. hands, And be one by the right hand of God.

Words: Patrick Prescod
Music: Noel Dexter
Copyright © 1981 Caribbean Conference of Churches

JESUS CHRIST OUR LORD

In Christ There Is No East or West

1. In Christ there is no East or West, In
2. In Him shall true hearts ev - ery - where Their
3. Join hands, di - ci - ples of the faith, What
4. In Christ now meet both East and West, In

1. Him no South or North; But one great fel - low -
2. high com - mu - nion find; His ser - vice is the
3. e'er your race may be! Who serves my Fa - ther
4. Him meet South and North; All Christ - ly souls are

1. ship of love Through - out the whole wide earth.
2. gold - en cord Close - bind - ing hu - man kind.
3. as a son Is sure - ly kin to me.
4. one in him Through out the whole wide earth.

Words: Galatians 3:28; adapt. John Oxenham (1852-1941)
Music: *McKee*, Negro Spiritual; adapt. Harry T. Burleigh (1866-1949)
Words adapt. Copyright © 1989. Reprinted by permission of American Tract Society.
Music Used by Permission.

Glo - rious is the Name of Je - sus, Prais - es to His

Name. Oh, ___ glo - rious and ___ right - eous and ___

Ho - ly is His Name. Oh, __ glo - ri - ous is __ His

Name. _____ I feel His pres - ence

Words: Robert J. Fryson
Music: Robert J. Fryson
Copyright © 1982 Robert J. Fryson, D.Min.

I Love To Tell the Story

1. I love to tell the sto - ry Of un - seen things a - bove,
2. I love to tell the sto - ry, For those who know it best

1. Of Je - sus and His glo - ry, Of _ Je - sus and His love.
2. Seem hun - ger-ing and thirst-ing To hear it, like the rest.

1. I love to tell the sto - ry, Be - cause I know it's true;
2. And when, in scenes of glo - ry, I sing the new, new song,

1. It sat - is-fies my long-ings As noth-ing else would do.
2. 'Twill be the old, old sto - ry That I have loved so long.

I love to tell the sto - ry; 'Twill be my theme in glo - ry.

Words: A. Katherine Hankey (1831-1911)
Music: William G. Fischer (1835-1912)

To tell the old, old sto-ry Of Je-sus and His love.

Bless The Lord, O My Soul 65

Bless the Lord, __ O my soul: and all that is with-

in me, Bless His ho - ly __ name. __

Fine

He has done great things, ____ He has done great __

D.C.

things, __ He has done great things, Bless His ho - ly name!

Words: Psalm 103:1
Music: Andrae Crouch (b. 1942)
Copyright © Bud John Songs, Inc./ASCAP

I Must Tell Jesus

1. I must tell Je - sus all of my tri - als; I can - not
2. I must tell Je - sus all of my trou - bles, He is a
3. Tempt - ed and tried I need a great Sav - ior, One who can
4. O how the world to e - vil al - lures me! O how my

1. bear these bur - dens a - lone, In my dis - tress He kind - ly will
2. kind, com - pas - sion - ate friend; If I but ask Him, He will de -
3. help my bur - dens to bear; I must tell Je - sus, I must tell
4. heart is tempt - ed to sin! I must tell Je - sus, and He will

1. help me, He ev - er loves and cares for His own.
2. liv - er, Make of my trou - bles quick - ly an end.
3. Je - sus; He all my cares and sor - rows will share.
4. help me, O - ver the world the vic - t'ry to win.

I must tell Je - sus! I must tell Je - sus! I can - not

bear my bur - dens a - lone; I must tell Je - sus! I must tell

Words: Elisha A. Hoffman (1839-1929)
Music: Elisha A. Hoffman

Je - sus! Je - sus can help me, Je - sus a - lone.

I Love the Lord

67

1. I love the Lord, _____ He heard my
2. I love the Lord, _____ He heard my

1. cry _____ and pit - ied ev - 'ry groan.
2. cry _____ and pit - ied ev - 'ry groan. _____

1. __ Long as I live _____ and trou - bles rise, _____
2. __ O let my heart _____ no more des - pair _____

1. __ I'll has - ten to _____ His throne.
2. __ while I have breath _____ to pray.

Words: Traditional
Music: Traditional; arr. Richard Smallwood
Arr. used by permission of Century Oak/Richwood Music.

I've Decided to Make Jesus My Choice

1. Some folk would rather have houses and land.
2. These clothes may be ragged that I'm wearing.

1. Some folk choose silver and gold.
2. Heavy is the load that I'm bearing.

1. These things they treasure and forget about their
2. These old burdens that I'm car —

1. soul; I've decided to make Jesus my choice.
2. rying

Words: Harris Johnson
Music: Harris Johnson

The road is rough, the go - ing gets tough, and the hills are hard to climb,____ I've start - ed out a long time a - go, there's no doubt in my mind; I've de - cid - ed____ to make Je - sus my choice.____

In the Garden

1. I come to the gar-den a-lone, _____ While the
2. He speaks, and the sound of His voice _____ Is so
3. I'd stay in the gar-den with Him _____ Though the

1. dew is still on the ros - es; And the voice I hear, fall - ing
2. sweet the birds hush their sing - ing; And the me - lo - dy that He
3. night a-round me be fall - ing; But He bids me go through the

1. on my ear, The Son of God dis - clos - es.
2. gave to me With - in my heart is ring - ing.
3. voice of woe, His voice to me is call - ing.

And He walks with me, and He talks with me, And He

tells me I am His own, _____ And the joy we share as we

Words: C. Austin Miles (1868-1946)
Music: C. Austin Miles

tar - ry there, None oth - er has ev - er___ known. ___

I Want Jesus to Walk with Me

70

1. I want Je - sus___ to walk with me (walk with me); I want
2. In my tri - als, ___ Lord, walk with me (walk with me); In my
3. In my sor - rows, ___ Lord, walk with me (walk with me); In my

1. Je - sus___ to walk_ with me (walk with me); All a
2. tri - als, ___ Lord, walk_ with me (walk with me); When the
3. sor - rows, ___ Lord, walk_ with me (walk with me); When my

1. long my___ pil - grim jour - ney, ___ Lord, I want
2. shades of___ life___ are fall - ing, ___ Lord, I want
3. heart with - in___ is ach - ing, ___ Lord, I want

1. Je - sus___ to walk with me (walk with me).
2. Je - sus___ to walk with me (walk with me).
3. Je - sus___ to walk with me (walk with me).

Words: Traditional
Music: Negro Spiritual; arr. Carl Haywood (b. 1949), from *The Haywood Collection of Negro Spirituals*,
Copyright © 1992.

In Times Like These

1, 2. Your an-chor holds _____ and grips the Sol - id Rock! _____
3. My an-chor holds _____ and grips the Sol - id Rock! _____

Just a Closer Walk with Thee 72

1. I am weak but thou art strong; _____
2. Through this world of toil and snares, _____
3. When my fee - ble life is o'er, _____

Refrain: Just a clos - er walk with thee, _____

1. Je - sus, keep me from all wrong; __ I'll be sat - is - fied as
2. If I fal - ter, Lord, who cares? __ Who with me my bur - den
3. Time for me will be no more; __ Guide me gent - ly, safe - ly

Refrain: Grant it, Je - sus, is my plea, _____ Dai - ly walk-ing close to

D.C. for Refrain

1. long _____ As I walk, let me walk close to thee.
2. shares? __ None but thee, dear __ Lord, none but thee.
3. o'er _____ To Thy king - dom __ shore, to thy shore.

Refrain: thee, _____ Let it be, dear __ Lord, let it be.

Words: Anonymous
Music: American Folk Song

Is There Anybody Here Who Loves My Jesus?

Is there an - y - bod - y here who loves my Je - sus?

An - y - bod - y here who loves my Lord? __ I want to know if you

love __ my __ Je - sus; I want to know if you love __ my __ Lord.

Fine

1. This __ world's a ____ wil - der - ness __ of ____ woe,
2. Re - li - gion __ is a ____ bloom - ing __ rose,
3. When __ I ____ was __ blind and ___ could __ not ___ see.
4. When __ ev - 'ry __ star re - fus - es to ____ shine,

D.C.

1. So ____ let ____ us ____ all to glo - ry ___ go.
2. And __ none ___ but __ them who feel ___ it ____ know.
3. King __ Je - sus __ brought the light ___ to ___ me.
4. I ____ know __ King __ Je - sus will ___ be ___ mine.

Words: Traditional
Music: Negro Spiritual

Je - su, _____ Je - su, _____ fill us with your love, show

us how to serve the neigh-bors we have from you. _____

Fine

1. Kneels at the feet of his friends, si - lent - ly wash-es their
2. Neigh-bors are rich ___ and poor, neigh-bors are black ___ and
3. These are the ones we should serve, these are the ones we should
4. Lov - ing puts us on our knees, serv - ing as though we are
5. Kneel at the feet of our friends, si - lent - ly wash-ing their

D.C.

1. feet, Mas - ter who acts as a slave ___ to them. ___
2. white, neigh-bors are near ___ and far ___ a - way. ___
3. love; all these are neigh-bors to us ___ and you. ___
4. slaves, this is the way we should live ___ with you. ___
5. feet, this is the way we should live ___ with you. ___

Words: John 13:1-17; adapt. Tom Colvin, 1969
Music: Ghana Folk Song; adapt. Tom Colvin, 1969; harm. Charles H. Webb, 1988

Jesu, Joy of Our Desiring

1. Je - su, Joy of our de - sir - ing, Ho - ly wis - dom love most bright.
2. This the way where hope is guid - ing, Hear what peace - ful mu - sic rings.

1. Drawn by thee our souls as - pir - ing, Soar to un - cre - a - ted light.
2. Where the flock in thee con - fi - ding, Drink of joy from breath - less springs.

1. Word of God our flesh that fash - ioned. With the fire of, life im - pas - sioned.
2. Theirs is beau - ty's fair - est pleas - ure. Theirs is wis - doms ho - liest trea - sures.

1. Striv - ing still to truth un - known, Soar - ing, dy - ing 'round thy throne.
2. Thou dost ev - er lead thine own, In the love of joys un - known.

Words: Martin Janus
Music: William B. Cooper

Jesus in the Morning

1. Je - sus, Je - sus, Je - sus in the morn - ing
2. Praise __ Him, Praise __ Him, Praise Him in the morn - ing
3. Love __ Him, Love __ Him, Love Him in the morn - ing
4. Serve __ Him, Serve __ Him, Serve Him in the morn - ing
5. Je - sus, Je - sus, Je - sus in the morn - ing

1. Je - sus in the noon - time; Je - sus,
2. Praise Him in the noon - time; Praise __ Him,
3. Love Him in the noon - time; Love __ Him,
4. Serve Him in the noon - time; Serve __ Him,
5. Je - sus in the noon - time; Je - sus,

1. Je - sus, Je - sus when the sun goes down!
2. Praise __ Him, Praise Him when the sun goes down!
3. Love __ Him, Love Him when the sun goes down!
4. Serve __ Him, Serve Him when the sun goes down!
5. Je - sus, Je - sus when the sun goes down!

Words: Traditional
Music: Negro Spiritual

1. Je - sus is all the world to me. My life, my joy, my all; ____ He is my strength from day to day, With-out Him I ____ would fall: ____ When I am sad, to Him I go. No oth-er one can cheer me so;
2. Je - sus is all the world to me, My friend in tri - als sore; ____ I go to Him for bless - ings, and He gives them o'er __ and o'er; ____ He sends the sun - shine and the rain. He sends the har - vest's gold - en grain;
3. Je - sus is all the world to me, And true to Him I'll be; ____ Oh, how could I this friend de - ny, When He's so true __ to me? ____ Fol - low-ing Him I know I'm right. He watch-es o'er me day and night;
4. Je - sus is all the world to me, I want no bet - ter friend; ____ I trust Him now, I'll trust Him when Life's fleet - ing days __ shall end: ____ Beau - ti - ful life with such a friend. Beau - ti - ful life that has no end;

Words: Will L. Thompson (1847-1909)
Music: Will L. Thompson

1. When I am sad He makes me glad, He's my friend. __
2. Sun - shine and rain, har - vest of grain, He's my friend. __
3. Fol - low - ing Him by day and night, He's my friend. __
4. E - ter - nal life, e - ter - nal joy, He's my friend. __

Blessed Be the Name 78

1. Bless - ed be the name! Bless - ed be the name! Bless - ed be the name of the Lord! Bless - ed be the name! Bless - ed be the name! Bless - ed be the name of the Lord!

2. Jesus is the
   name of the Lord!

3. Worthy to be grand
   is the Lord!

Words: Psalm 72:19
Music: Campmeeting Melody; arr. Ralph E. Hudson, 1887

Jesus, Lover of My Soul

1. Je - sus, lov - er of my soul, Let me to thy bo - som fly,
2. Oth - er ref - uge have I none, Hangs my help - less soul on thee;
3. Plen - teous grace with thee is found, Grace to cleanse from ev - 'ry sin;

1. While the near - er wa - ters roll, While the tem - pest still is high;
2. Leave, ah! leave me not a - lone, Still sup - port and com - fort me!
3. Let the heal - ing streams a - bound, Make and keep me pure with - in.

1. Hide me, O my Sa - vior, hide, Till the storm of life be past;
2. All my trust on thee is stayed; All my help from thee I bring;
3. Thou of life the foun - tain art, Free - ly let me take of thee:

1. Safe in - to the ha - ven guide, O re - ceive my soul at last.
2. Cov - er my de - fence - less head With the sha - dow of thy wing.
3. Spring thou up with - in my heart, Rise to all e - ter - ni - ty.

Words: Charles Wesley (1707-1788)
Music: Charles Wesley and Simeon B. Marsh (1798-1875)

Jesus, Savior, Pilot Me

1. Je - sus, Sav - ior, pi - lot me, O - ver life's tem -
2. As a moth - er stills— her child, Thou canst hush the
3. When at last I near— the shore, And the fear - ful

1. pes - tuous sea: Un - known waves be - fore me roll, ——
2. o - cean wild; Bois - t'rous waves o - bey thy will ——
3. break - ers roar 'Twixt me and the peace - ful rest ——

1. Hid - ing rocks and treach - 'rous shoal; Chart and com - pass
2. When thou say'st to them, "Be still!" Won - drous Sov - 'reign
3. Then, while lean - ing on thy breast, May I hear thee

1. come — from thee, Je - sus, Sav - ior, pi - lot me!
2. of —— the sea, Je - sus, Sav - ior, pi - lot me!
3. say —— to me, "Fear not- I will pi - lot thee!"

Words: Edward Hopper (1816-1888)
Music: John E. Gould (1822-1875)

Jesus, We Want to Meet

1. Je - sus, we want — to meet On this — thy ho - ly day;
2. We kneel in awe — and fear On this — thy ho - ly day;
3. Thy bless - ing, Lord, — we seek On this — thy ho - ly day;
4. Our minds we ded - i - cate On this — thy ho - ly day;

1. We gath - er round — thy throne On this — thy ho - ly day.
2. Pray God to teach — us here On this — thy ho - ly day.
3. Give joy of thy vic - to - ry On this — thy ho - ly day.
4. Heart and soul con - se - crate On this — thy ho - ly day.

1. Thou — art — our heaven - ly Friend, Hear our prayers as they as - cend;
2. Save — us — and cleanse our hearts, Lead and guide our acts of praise,
3. Through grace a - lone are we saved; In thy flock may we be found;
4. Ho - ly Spir - it make us whole; Bless the ser - mon in this place;

1. Look in - to our hearts and minds to - day, On this — thy ho - ly day.
2. And our faith from seed to flow - er raise, On this — thy ho - ly day.
3. Let the mind of Christ a - bide in us On this — thy ho - ly day.
4. And — as we go, — lead us Lord; On this — thy ho - ly day.

Words: A. T. Olajide, 1949; tr. Biodun Adebesin; verses, Austin C. Lovelace, 1962.
Music: Nigerian Folk Song; tr. A. T. Olajide; harm. Carl Haywood (b. 1949), from *Songs of Praise*, Harm. Copyright
© 1992. Tr. and Versification Copyright © 1964 Abingdon Press. Reprinted from *The Book of Hymns* by permission.

1. Just when I need Him, Je - sus is near,
2. Just when I need Him, Je - sus is true,
3. Just when I need Him, Je - sus is strong,
4. Just when I need Him, He is my all,

1. Just when I fal - ter, just when I fear; Read - y to help me,
2. Ne - ver for - sak - ing all the way through; Giv - ing for bur - dens
3. Bear - ing my bur - dens all the day long; For all my sor - row
4. An - swer - ing when up - on Him I call; Ten - der - ly watch - ing

1. read - y to cheer, Just when I need Him most.
2. plea - sures a - new, Just when I need Him most.
3. giv - ing a song, Just when I need Him most.
4. lest I should fall, Just when I need Him most.

Just when I need Him most, Just when I need Him most;

Je - sus is near to com - fort and cheer, Just when I need Him most.

Words: William C. Poole (1875-1949)
Music: Charles H. Gabriel (1856-1932)

Just a Little Talk With Jesus

1. I once was lost in sin but Jesus took me in,
2. Sometimes my path seems drear, without a ray of cheer,
3. I may have doubts and fears, my eyes be filled with tears,

1. And then a little light from heaven filled my soul;
2. And then a cloud of doubt may hide the light of day;
3. But Jesus is a friend who watches day and night;

1. It bathed my heart in love and wrote my name above,
2. The mists of sin may rise and hide the starry skies,
3. I go to Him in pray'r, He knows my ev'ry care.

1. And just a little talk with Jesus made me whole.
2. And just a little talk with Jesus clears the way.
3. And just a little talk with Jesus makes it right.

King Jesus Is a-Listenin'

King Jesus is a-lis-ten-in' all day long, King Jesus is a-lis-ten-in' all day long, King Je-sus is a lis-ten-in' all day long, To hear some sin-ner pray.

1. That Gos-pel train is com-in', A - rum-blin' through the lan', But I hear them wheels a - hum-min', Get read - y to board that train!
2. I know I been con - vert - ed, I ain't gon' make no a - larm, For my soul is bound for glo - ry, And the dev-il can't do me no harm.
3. Some say that John the Bap - tist was noth - in' but a Jew, But the Ho - ly Bi - ble tells us That John was a preach - er too.

Fine

D.C.

Words: Traditional
Music: Negro Spiritual; arr. Carl Haywood (b. 1949), from *The Haywood Collection of Negro Spirituals*,
Copyright © 1992.

Let all that is with-in me ___ cry, 1. "Ho - ly!" Let
2. "Bless - ed!"
3. "Wor - thy!"

all that is with-in me ___ cry, 1."Ho - ly!" Ho - ly!
2."Bless - ed!" Bless - ed!
3."Wor - thy!" Wor - thy!

1. Ho - ly! Ho - ly is the Lamb that was slain. _____
2. Bless - ed! Bless - ed is the Lamb that was slain. _____
3. Wor - thy! Wor - thy is the Lamb that was slain. _____

Words: Tr. by Melvin Harrel
Music: Anonymous; arr. Charles High

Let Jesus Fix It for You

1. If ____ your life in days gone by, Has not been good and true, ____
2. Per-haps your tem-per is to blame, For man-y wrongs you do, ____
3. If in your home the trou-ble is, The course you should pur-sue, ____
4. And if some sin your soul hath bound With cords you can't un-do, ____
5. May-be to you the world is dark, And com-forts far and few, ____

1. In your own way no long-er try, But let Him fix it for you. ____
2. Take it to God in Je-sus' name, And He will fix it for you. ____
3. Go talk with God, your hand in His, And He will fix it for you. ____
4. At Je-sus' feet go lay it down, And He will fix it for you. ____
5. Let Je-sus own and rule your heart, And He will fix it for you. ____

Let Je-sus fix it for you, ____ He knows just what to do; ____

When-ev-er you pray, let Him have His way, And He will fix it for you. ____

Words: Charles A. Tindley (1851-1933)
Music: Charles A. Tindley; arr. Frederick J. Tindley

More Love to Thee, O Christ

87

1. More love to thee, O Christ, More love to thee!
2. Once earth-ly joy I craved, Sought peace and rest;
3. Then shall my ev-ery breath Sing out your praise;

1. Hear thou the prayer I make On bend-ed knee;
2. Now thee a-lone I seek, Give what is best;
3. This be the on-ly song My heart shall raise;

1. This is my ear-nest plea;
2. This all my prayer shall be: More love, O Christ, to Thee,
3. This still my prayer shall be:

More love to thee, More love to thee!

Words: Elizabeth P. Prentiss (1818-1878)
Music: William H. Doane (1832-1915)

My Faith Looks up to Thee

1. My faith looks up to thee, Thou lamb of
2. May thy rich grace im - part Strength to my
3. While life's dark maze I tread, And griefs a -
4. When ends life's tran - sient dream, When death's cold,

1. Cal - va - ry, Sav - ior di - vine!
2. faint - ing heart, My zeal in - spire;
3. round me spread, Be thou my guide;
4. sul - len stream Shall o'er me roll;

1. Now hear me while I pray, Take all my guilt a - way;
2. As thou hast died for me, O may my love to thee
3. Bid dark-ness turn to-day, Wipe so-row's tears a - way;
4. Blest Sav-ior, then in love, Fear and dis - trust re-move,

1. O let me from this day Be whol - ly thine.
2. Pure, warm, and change - less be A liv - ing fire.
3. Not let me ev - er stray From thee a - side.
4. O bear me safe a-bove, A ran - somed soul.

Words: Ray Palmer (1808-1887)
Music: Lowell Mason (1792-1872)

1. My Je - sus, I love ___ thee, I know thou art mine,
2. I love thee be - cause ___ thou hast first lov - ed me,
3. I'll love thee in life, ___ I will love thee in death,
4. In man - sions of glo - ry and end - less de - light,

1. For thee all the fol - lies of sin I re - sign;
2. And pur - chased my par - don on Cal - va - ry's tree;
3. And praise thee as long ___ as thou lend - est me breath;
4. I'll ev - er a - dore ___ thee in heav - en so bright;

1. My gra - cious Re - deem - er, my Sav - ior art thou: ___
2. I love thee for wear - ing the thorns ___ on thy brow: ___
3. And say when the death - dew lies cold ___ on my brow, ___
4. I'll sing with the glit - ter - ing crown ___ on my brow, ___

1. If ev - er I loved ___ thee, my Je - sus, 'tis now.
2. If ev - er I loved ___ thee, my Je - sus, 'tis now.
3. "If ev - er I loved ___ thee, my Je - sus, 'tis now."
4. "If ev - er I loved ___ thee, my Je - sus, 'tis now."

Words: William R. Featherstone (1846-1873)
Music: Adoniram J. Gordon (1836-1895)

No, Not One!

1. There's not a friend like the low - ly Je - sus,
2. No friend like Him is so high and ho - ly,
3. There's not an hour that He is not near us,
4. Did ev - er saint find this Friend for - sake Him?
5. Was e'er a gift like the Sav - ior giv - en?

1. No, not one! no, not one! None else could heal all our
2. No, not one! no, not one! And yet no friend is so
3. No, not one! no, not one! No night so dark but His
4. No, not one! no, not one! Or sin - ner find that He
5. No, not one! no, not one! Will He re - fuse us a

1. soul's dis - eas - es, No, not one! no, not one!
2. meek and low - ly, No, not one! no, not one!
3. love can cheer us, No, not one! no, not one!
4. would not take him? No, not one! no, not one!
5. home in heav - en? No, not one! no, not one!

Je - sus knows all a - bout our strug - gles, He will guide till the day is done;

Words: Johnson Oatman, Jr. (1856-1922)
Music: George C. Hugg (1848-1907)

There's not a friend like the low-ly Je-sus, No, not one! no not one!

Give Me Jesus 91

1. In the morn-ing when I rise, In the morn-ing when I
2. Dark __ mid-night was my cry Dark __ mid-night was my
3. O ___ when I come to die, O ___ when I come to

1. rise, In the morn-ing when I rise, Give me Je - - sus.
2. cry, Dark __ mid-night was my cry, Give me Je - - sus.
3. die, O ___ when I come to die Give me Je - - sus.

Give me Je - sus, Give me Je - sus, You may

have all this world, Give me Je - sus.

Words: Traditional
Music: Negro Spiritual; arr. Evelyn D. White. Used by Permission.

Nothing Between

1. Noth-ing be-tween my soul and the Sav - ior, Naught of this world's de-
2. Noth-ing be-tween like world - ly plea-sure, Hab - its of life though
3. Noth-ing be-tween like pride or sta-tion: Self or friends shall
4. Noth-ing be-tween e'en man-y hard tri - als, Though the whole world a-

1. lu - sive dreams; I have re-nounced all sin - ful plea-sure,
2. harm-less they seem, Must not my heart from Him ev - er sev - er,
3. not in - ter-vene; Though it may cost me much trib - u - la-tion,
4. gainst me con - vene; Watch-ing with prayer and much self de - ni - al.

1. Je - sus is mine, There's noth-ing be - tween.
2. He is my all! There's noth-ing be - tween.
3. I am re-solved! There's noth-ing be - tween.
4. Tri-umph at last, with noth-ing be - tween.

Noth-ing be - tween my

soul and the Sav - ior, So that His bless - ed face may be seen;

Words: Charles A. Tindley (1851-1933)
Music: Charles A. Tindley; arr. J. Edward Hoy (b. 1920)

Noth-ing pre-vent-ing the least of His fa-vor: Keep the way clear! Let noth-ing be-tween.

Give Thanks to the Lord 93

Give thanks to the Lord for He is so good, His mer-cy en-

1. dures for-ev-er (for-ev-er.) Give dures for-ev-er. (for-

Fine

ev-er.) 1. To Him a-lone who does might-y won-ders,
2. He made the sun to gov-ern the day-time,

D.C.

1. Who by His un-der-stand-ing made the hea - vens.
2. The moon and stars to gov-ern o'er the night - time.

Words: Brenda Barker (b. 1959)
Music: Ken Barker (b. 1955) and Debi Parker Ladd (b. 1961)

O Holy Savior!

1. O ho - ly Sav - ior! friend un - seen, Since on thine arm thou bid'st me lean, Help me, through - out life's chang - ing scene, By faith to cling to thee.

2. What though the world de - ceit - ful prove, And earth - ly friends and joys re - move? With pa - tient un - comp - lain - ing love, Still I would cling to thee.

3. Though faith and hope a - while be tried, I ask not, need not aught be - side: How safe, how calm, how sat - is - fied, The souls that cling to thee.

1. There is a name I love to hear, I love to sing its worth;
2. It tells me of a Savior's love, Who died to set me free;
3. It tells me what my Father hath In store for ev-'ry day,
4. It tells of one whose loving heart Can feel my deepest woe,

1. It sounds like music in mine ear, The sweetest name on earth.
2. It tells me of His precious blood, The sinner's perfect plea.
3. And though I tread a darksome path, Yields sunshine all the way.
4. Who in each sorrow bears a part, That none can bear below.

O how I love Jesus, O how I love Jesus,

O how I love Jesus, Because He first loved me!

Words: Frederick Whitfield (1829-1904)
Music: American Melody

He Is King of Kings

He is King of kings, He is Lord of Lords;

Je - sus Christ, the first and last __ no man works like Him. He is

no man works like Him. 1. He built his throne up in the air __
2. I was but young when I be - gun __

no man works like Him; 1. And called the saints from
2. But now my race is

1. ev - 'er where __ no man works like Him. He is
2. al - most won __

Words: Traditional
Music: Negro Spiritual; arr. Horace Clarence Boyer (b. 1935)
Arr. Copyright © 1992 Horace Clarence Boyer

Ride on, King Jesus

Words: Traditional
Music: Negro Spiritual; arr. Hezekiah Brinson, Jr. (b. 1958)

Praise Him

1. ris - ing of the _____ sun un - til the
2. God _____ is our _____ rock, hope of sal -
3. ris - ing of the _____ sun un - til the

1. go - ing down of the _____ same; He's wor - thy, Je- sus is
2. va - tion; A strong _____ de - li - ver -
3. go - ing down of the _____ same; He's wor - thy, Je- sus is

D.S.

1. wor - thy, He's wor-thy to _____ be praised.
2. er, _____ In Him I will al- ways trust.
3. wor - thy, He's wor-thy to _____ be praised.

1. My hope is built on noth-ing less Than Je-sus' blood and
2. When dark-ness veils His love-ly face, I rest on His un -
3. His oath, His cov - e - nant and blood, Sup - port me in the
4. When He shall come with trum-pet sound, O may I then in

1. right - eous-ness; I dare not trust the sweet-est frame, But
2. chang - ing grace; In ev - 'ry high and storm-y gale, My
3. whelm-ing flood; When all a - round my soul gives way, He
4. Him be found; Dressed in His right - eous - ness a - lone, Fault -

1. whol - ly lean on Je-sus' name.
2. an - chor holds with - in the veil. On Christ, the so - lid Rock, I stand, All
3. then is all my hope and stay.
4. less to stand be - fore the throne.

oth-er ground is sink-ing sand, All oth-er ground is sink-ing sand.

Words: Edward Mote (1797-1874)
Music: William B. Bradbury (1816-1868)

Somebody's Knockin' at Your Door

Softly and Tenderly Jesus Is Calling

1. Soft - ly and ten - der - ly Je - sus is call - ing,
2. Why should we tar - ry when Je - sus is plead - ing,
3. Time is now fleet - ing, the mo - ments are pass - ing,
4. Oh! for the won - der - ful love He has prom - ised,

1. Call - ing for you and for me; See, on the por - tals He's
2. Plead-ing for you and for me? Why should we lin - ger and
3. Pass - ing for you and for me; Shad - ows are gath - er - ing,
4. Prom-ised for you and for me; Though we have sinned, He has

1. wait - ing and watch-ing, Watch-ing for you and for me.
2. heed not His mer - cies, Mer - cies for you and for me?
3. death beds are com - ing, Com - ing for you and for me.
4. mer - cy and par - don, Par - don for you and for me.

Come home, come home,
Come home, come home,

Words: Will L. Thompson (1847-1909)
Music: Will L. Thompson

Ye who are wea-ry, come home!____ Ear-nest-ly, ten-der-ly,

Je-sus is call-ing, Call-ing, O sin-ner, come home!____

O I Love Him

102

Harmony

O ____ I love Him, ____ O ____ I love Him ____ be-

cause He ____ first ____ loved me, first loved me.

Hymn continues on the next page.

Words: Phillip McIntyre (1952-1991)
Music: Phillip McIntyre
Copyright © Phillip McIntyre. Permission Requested.

Steal a-way, steal a-way, steal a-way to Je-sus!

Fine

Steal a-way, steal a-way home, I ain't got long to stay here!

1. My Lord___ calls me, He calls me by the thun-der;
2. Green trees are bend-ing, Poor sin-ner stands a-trem-bling;
3. Tomb stones are burst-ing, Poor sin-ner stands a-trem-bling;
4. My Lord___ calls me, He calls me by the light-ning,

D.C.

The trum-pet sounds with-in-a my soul, I ain't got long to stay here.

Words: Traditional
Music: Negro Spiritual; arr. Edward C. Deas
Arr. Copyright © Sunday School Publishing Board

The Lord Is My Shepherd

1. The Lord is my Shep-herd, no want shall I know;
2. Through the val-ley and shad-ow my death though I stray,
3. In the midst of af-flic-tion my ta-ble is spread;
4. Let good-ness and mer-cy, my boun-ti-ful God,

1. I feed in green pas-tures, safe-fold-ed I rest; —
2. Since thou art my guard-ian, no e-vil I fear; —
3. With bless-ings un-meas-ured my cup run-neth o'er; —
4. Still fol-low my steps till I meet Thee a-bove; —

1. He lead-eth my soul where the still wa-ters flow, —
2. Thy rod shall de-fend me, thy staff be my stay; —
3. With per-fume and oil thou a-nount-est my head; —
4. I seek by the path which my an-ces-tors trod, —

1. Re - stores me when wan-d'ring, re-deems when op-pressed;
2. No harm can be-fall, with my com-fort-er near;
3. O what shall I ask of thy prov-i-dence more?
4. Through the land of their so-journ, thy king-dom of love;

Words: James Montgomery (1771-1854)
Music: Thomas Koschat (1845-1914)

1. Re - stores me when wan-d'ring, re-deems when op-pressed.
2. No ___ harm can be-fall, with my com-fort-er near.
3. O ___ what shall I ask of thy prov-i-dence more?
4. Through the land of their so-journ, thy king-dom of love.

I'm So Glad, Jesus Lifted Me

1. I'm so glad ___ Je-sus lift-ed me ___ I'm so glad ___
glad that lift-ed so glad that
Je-sus lift-ed me. ___ I'm so glad, ___ Je-sus lift-ed me _ sing-ing
Lord so glad that
glo - ry Hal - le-lu - jah ___ Je - sus lift - ed me. _

2. Satan had me bound (Jesus lifted me).   3. When I was in sin (Jesus lifted me).

Words: Traditional
Music: Negro Spiritual; arr. Hezekiah Brinson, Jr. (b. 1958)

Take My Hand, Precious Lord

1. Pre - cious Lord, take my hand, Lead me on, let me
2. When my way grows_ drear, pre - cious Lord, lin - ger
3. When the dark - ness ap - pears and the night draws_

1. stand, _ I am tired, I am weak, I am worn;_____
2. near, _ When my life is _ al - most _ gone;_____
3. near, _ And the day is _ past and _ gone;_____

1. _ Through the storm, through the night, Lead me on to the
2. _ Hear my cry, hear my call, Hold my hand, lest I
3. _ At the riv - er I stand, Guide my feet, hold my

1. light, _ Take my hand, pre - cious Lord, _ Lead me on._____
2. fall, _ Take my hand, pre - cious Lord, _ Lead me on._____
3. hand, _ Take my hand, pre - cious Lord, _ Lead me on._____

Words: Thomas A. Dorsey (1899–1993)
Music: Thomas A. Dorsey (1899–1993); arr. Horace Clarence Boyer (b. 1935)

There's Something About That Name

Words: Gloria (b. 1942) and William Gaither (b. 1936)
Music: William J. Gaither

'Tis So Sweet to Trust Jesus

1. 'Tis so sweet to trust in Je-sus, Just to take Him at His word.
2. O how sweet to trust in Je-sus, Just to trust His cleans-ing blood.
3. Yes, 'tis sweet to trust in Je-sus, Just from sin and self to cease.
4. I'm so glad I learned to trust thee, Pre-cious Je-sus, Sa-vior, Friend;

1. Just to rest up-on His prom-ise, Just to know, "Thus saith the Lord."
2. Just in sim-ple faith to plunge me 'Neath the heal-ing, cleans-ing flood!
3. Just from Je-sus sim-ply tak-ing Life and rest and joy and peace.
4. And I know that thou art with me, Wilt be with me to the end.

Je-sus, Je-sus, how I trust Him! How I've proved Him o'er and o'er!

Je-sus, Je-sus, pre-cious Je-sus! O for grace to trust Him more!

Words: Louisa M. R. Stead (1850-1917)
Music: William J. Kirkpatrick (1838-1921)

1. What a friend we have in Je - sus, All our sins and griefs to bear!
2. Have we tri - als and temp - ta - tions? Is there trou - ble an - y - where?
3. Are we weak and heav - y lad - en, Cum - bered with a load of care?

1. What a priv - i - ledge to car - ry Ev - 'ry - thing to God in prayer!
2. We should nev - er be dis - cour - aged, Take it to the Lord in prayer.
3. Pre - cious Sav - ior, still our ref - uge, Take it to the Lord in Prayer.

1. Oh, what peace we of - ten for - feit, Oh, what need - less pain we bear,
2. Can we find a friend so faith - ful who will all our sor - rows share?
3. Do thy friends de - spise, for - sake thee? Take it to the Lord in prayer.

1. All be - cause we do not car - ry Ev - 'ry - thing to God in prayer!
2. Je - sus knows our ev - 'ry weak - ness, Take it to the Lord in prayer.
3. In his arms He'll take and shield thee, Thou wilt find a sol - ace there.

Words: Joseph Scriven (1819-1866)
Music: Charles C. Converse (1832-1918)

You Hear the Lambs a-Cryin'

You hear the lambs a-cry-in', hear the lambs a cry-in',

hear the lambs a-cry-in' O Shep-herd, feed my sheep. You feed my sheep.

1. My Sav-ior spoke these words so sweet, say-in',

Oo_____ O Shep-herd, feed my sheep,

"Pe-ter, if you love me, feed my sheep."

Oo_____ O Shep-herd, feed my sheep. You

2. O Lord, I love thee, thou dost know;
O Shepherd, feed my sheep.
O give me grace to love thee more.
O Shepherd, feed my sheep.

3. O wasn't that an awful shame?
O Shepherd, feed my sheep.
He hung three hours in mortal pain.
O Shepherd, feed my sheep.

Words: Traditional
Music: Negro Spiritual; harm. Verolga Nix (b. 1933)
Harm. Copyright © 1981 Abingdon. Reprinted from *Songs of Zion* by permission.

HOLY SPIRIT

Come, Thou Fount of Every Blessing

1. Come, Thou fount of ev-ery bless-ing, Tune my heart to sing thy
2. Here I raise my Eb-en-e-zer, Hith-er by thy help I'm
3. O, to grace how great a debt-or, Dai-ly I'm con-strained to

1. grace; Streams of mer-cy nev-er ceas-ing, Call for songs of loud-est
2. come; And I hope, by thy good pleas-ure, Sure-ly to ar-rive at
3. be; Let that grace, Lord, like a fet-ter, Bind my won-d'ring heart to

1. praise. Teach me some me-lo-dious son-net, Sung by flam-ing tongues a
2. home. Je-sus sought me when a stran-ger, Wan-d'ring from the fold of
3. Thee. Prone to wan-der, Lord, I feel it, Prone to leave the God I

1. bove. Praise the mount, O fix me on it. Mount of God's un-chang-ing love.
2. God. He, to save my soul from dan-ger, In-ter-posed His pre-cious blood.
3. love. Here's my heart, Lord, take and seal it, Seal it from thy courts a-bove.

Words: Robert Robinson (1735-1790)
Music: *Nettleton*, melody from *A Repository of Sacred Music, Part II*, 1813; harm. Carl Haywood (b. 1949),
from *Songs of Praise*, Harm. Copyright © 1992.

Come, Holy Ghost

1. Come, Ho - ly Ghost, Cre - a - tor blest, And in our
2. O Com - fort - er, to thee we cry, Thou heav'n - ly
3. O Ho - ly Ghost, through thee a - lone, Know we the
4. Praise we the Lord, Fa - ther and Son, And Ho - ly

1. hearts___ take up___ thy rest; ___ Come with thy grace ___
2. gift___ of God ___ most high; ___ Thou fount of life, ___
3. Fa - ther and ___ the Son; ___ Be this our firm ___
4. Spir - it with ___ them one; ___ And may the Son ___

1. and heav'n - ly aid___ To fill the hearts ___ which ___ thou hast
2. and fire of love,___ And sweet a - noint - ing___ from a -
3. un - chang - ing creed,___ That thou dost from ___ them___ both pro -
4. on us be - stow___ All gifts that from ___ the ___ Spir - it

1. made, ___ To fill the hearts ___ which ___ thou ___ hast made.
2. bove, ___ And sweet a - nount - ing ___ from ___ a - bove.
3. ceed, ___ That thou dost from ___ them ___ both ___ pro - ceed.
4. flow, ___ All gifts that from ___ the ___ Spir - it flow.

Words: *Veni, Creator Spiritus*; attr. Rabanus Maurus, 776-856; tr. Edward Caswell (1814-1878), alt.
Music: *Lambillotte*, LM; with repeat; Louis Lambillotte, SJ (1796-1855); harm. Richard Proulx (b. 1937)
Harm. Copyright © 1992 G.I.A. Publications, Inc., Chicago, IL. All Rights Reserved.

1. How like a gentle spirit deep within,
2. Let God be God wher - ev - er life may be,
3. God like a moth - er ea - gle hov - ers near,
4. When in our vain pre - ten - sion we con - spire,

1. God reigns our fer - vent pas - sions day by day;
2. let ev - ery tongue bear wit - ness to the call;
3. on might - y wings of pow - er man - i - fest;
4. to shape God's im - age as we see our own;

1. and gives us strength to chal - lenge and to win,
2. all hu - man kind is one by God's de - cree,
3. God like a gen - tle shep - herd stills our fear,
4. hark to the voice a - bove our base de - sire,

1. de - spite the per - ils of our cho - sen way.
2. let God be God let God be God for all.
3. and com - forts us a - gainst a peace - ful breast.
4. God is the sculp - tor, we the bro - ken stone.

5. Through all our fretful claims of sex and race,
the universal love of God shines through;
for God is love transcending style and place,
and all the idle options we pursue.

Words: C. Eric Lincoln (1924-2000) © Lucy Cook Lincoln. Used by Permission.
Music: Edward John Hopkins (1818-1901)

Words: Traditional
Music: Negro Spiritual

1. fine,   asked__ my Lord   if all was   mine._____
2. track,   runs to heav - en and runs right back._____

Spirit of the Living God   115

Spir - it of the Liv - ing God, Fall fresh on   me,

Spir - it of the Liv - ing God, Fall fresh on   me.

Melt   me,   mold   me,   Fill   me,   use   me.

Spir - it of the Liv - ing God, Fall fresh on   me.

Words: Daniel Iverson (1890-1977)
Music: Daniel Iverson

Let It Breathe on Me

Let it breathe on me, ___ Let it breathe on me.

Let the breath of the Lord, now, breathe on ___ me,

Let it breathe on me. ___ Let it breathe on me.

Let the breath of the Lord, now, breathe on me.

1. While I'm work - ing Lord in your vine - yard here,
2. When the path - way Lord, I ___ can - not see,

1. I ___ can do naught if thou aren't near.
2. When the way is dark, Lord, breathe on me.

Words: Magnolia Lewis-Butts, 1942
Music: Magnolia Lewis-Butts; harm. W. O. Hoyle

1. Oh, ___ come, bless-ed Lord, just so close to me
2. Give me grace to ___ know when _ thou art near

1. That __ I may feel you breathe on me.
2. Oh, I pray thee, Lord, please breathe on me.

I'm Goin'-a Sing When the Spirit Says Sing   117

1. I'm goin' - a sing* when the Spir - it says sing. ____

I'm goin' - a sing when the Spir - it says sing. ____

I'm goin' - a sing when the Spir - it says sing, ___ and o -

bey the Spi - rit of the Lord. _____

* 2. pray 3. moan 4. shout

Words: Traditional
Music: Negro Spiritual; adapt. William Farley Smith (b. 1941)
Adapt Copyright © 1989 The United Methodist Publishing House. Reprinted from *The United Methodist Hymnal* by permission.

Spirit Song

1. Oh, let the Son of God en - fold you, __ with His
2. Oh, come and sing this song with glad - ness, __ as your

1. Spir - it and His love, Let Him fill your heart and
2. hearts are filled with joy, Lift your hands in sweet sur -

1. sat - is - fy __ your soul. __ Oh, let Him
2. ren - der to __ His name. __ Oh, give Him

1. have the things that hold you, __ and His Spir - it like a
2. all your tears and sad - ness, __ give Him all your years of

1. dove, Will de - scend up - on your life, and make you
2. pain, And you'll en - ter in - to life in Je - sus'

Words: John Wimber
Music: John Wimber

1. whole. _____ Je - sus. Oh,
2. name. _____

Je - sus, come and

fill your lambs. _____

Je - sus, Oh, Je - sus,

come and fill _____ your lambs. _____

Spirit of God, Descend upon My Heart

1. Spirit of God, descend upon my heart;
2. I ask no dream, no prophet ecstasies,
3. Teach me to feel that thou art always nigh;
4. Teach me to love thee as thine angels love.

1. Draw it from earth; through all its pulses move;
2. No sudden rending of the veil of clay,
3. Teach me the struggles of the soul to bear,
4. One holy passion filling all my frame;

1. Stoop to my weakness, mighty as thou art,
2. No angel visitant, no op'ning skies;
3. To check the rising doubt, the rebel sigh;
4. The kindling of the heav'n descended dove,

1. And make me love thee as I ought to love.
2. But take the dimness of my soul away.
3. Teach me the patience of unanswered prayer.
4. My heart an altar, and thy love the flame.

Words: George Croly (1780-1860)
Music: Frederick C. Atkinson (1841-1897)

Sweet, Sweet Spirit

1. There's a sweet, sweet Spir-it in this place, _____ And I
(2. There are) bless - ings you can-not re - ceive _____ Till you
(3. If you) say He saved you from your sin, _____ Now you're

1. know that it's the Spir - it of _ the Lord. _____ There are
2. know Him in His full - ness, and _ be - lieve. _____ You're the
3. weak, you're bound, and can - not en - ter in, _____ you can

Words: Doris Akers (b. 1922)
Music: Doris Akers

1. sweet ex - pres - sions on each face, _____ And I
2. one to pro - fit when you say, _____ "I am
3. make it right if you will yield; _____ You'll en -

1. know they feel the pres - ence of _ the Lord. _____
2. going to walk with Je - sus all _ the way." _____
3. joy the Ho - ly Spir - it that we feel. _____

Sweet Ho - ly Spir- it, Sweet Heav - en - ly Dove,

Stay right here with us,_____ fill-ing us with your love.

And for these bless-ings _____ we lift our hearts in

praise; With-out a doubt we'll know ___ that we have

been re - vived when we shall leave this place. 2. There are
3. If you place.

1.-2.
3.

BAPTISM AND CONVERSION

121

Baptized in Water

1. Bap-tized_ in wa-ter,__ sealed by the Spi-rit,__ Cleansed by the
2. Bap-tized_ in wa-ter,__ sealed by the Spi-rit,__ Dead in the
3. Bap-tized_ in wa-ter,__ sealed by the Spi-rit,__ Marked with the

1. blood of Christ __ our King: Heirs of sal-va-tion,__
2. tomb with Christ __ our King: One with his ris-ing.__
3. sign of Christ __ our King: Born of one Fa-ther,__

1. trust-ing his prom-ise,__ Faith-ful-ly now God's praise we sing.
2. freed and for-giv-en,__ Thank-ful-ly now God's praise we sing.
3. we are his child-ren,__ Joy-ful-ly now God's praise we sing.

Words: Michael Saward (b. 1932)
Music: Eugene Hancock (b. 1929)

Close to Thee

1. Thou my ev - er - last - ing por - tion, More than friend or life to me; All a - long my pil - grim jour - ney, Sav - ior, let me walk with thee. Close to thee, Close to Thee, Close to thee, Close to thee; All a - long my pil - grim jour - ney, Sav - ior, let me walk with thee.

2. Not for ease or world - ly pleas - ure, Nor for fame my prayer shall be; Glad - ly will I toil and suf - fer, On - ly let me walk with thee. Close to thee, Close to Thee, Close to thee, Close to thee; Glad - ly will I toil and suf - fer, On - ly let me walk with thee.

3. Lead me through the vale of shad - ows, Bear me o'er life's fit - ful sea; Then the gate of life e - ter - nal May I en - ter, Lord, with thee. Close to thee, Close to Thee, Close to thee, Close to thee; Then the gate of life e - ter - nal May I en - ter, Lord, with thee.

Words: Fanny J. Crosby (1820-1915)
Music: Silas Vail (1818-1884)

Done Made My Vow

Done made my vow to the Lord, And I
nev - er will turn back, Oh I will go,_____ I
shall go to see what the end will be.

1. Some - times I'm __ up, some - times I'm down;__ See what the end will be, But
2. When I was a mourn - er just like you;__ See what the end will be, I

1. still my soul is heav'n - ly bound, __ See what the end will be.
2. prayed and prayed 'til I came through, __ See what the end will be.

Words: Traditional
Music: Negro Spiritual; arr. Evelyn Davidson White. Used by Permission.

Give Me a Clean Heart

Give me a clean heart so I may serve

Thee. Lord, fix my heart ____ so that I ____ may be used ____ by

thee. For I'm not wor - thy of all these bless -

Hymn continues on the next page.

ings. Give me a clean heart_____ and I'll fol-low thee _____

_____ 1. I'm not ask - ing for the rich - es of the land. _____
(2. Some-times) I am up and some-times I am down. _____

1. _____ I'm not ask - ing for the proud to know my
2. _____ Some - times I am al - most lev - el to the

1. name. _____ Please _ give me, Lord, a clean heart, that
2. ground. _____ Please _ give me, Lord, a clean heart, that

1. I may fol - low thee. Give me a clean heart, a
2. I may fol - low thee. Give me a clean heart, a

1. clean heart and I will fol - low thee. _____ 2. Some - times
2. clean heart and I will fol - low thee. _____

Fix Me, Jesus

Oh, _____ fix me; Oh, _____ fix me;
Je - sus Je - sus

Fine

Oh, _____ fix me; fix me, Je - sus, fix me.

1. Fix me for _ my long white robe.
2. Fix me for _ my jour - ney home.
Fix me, Je - sus, fix me.

D.C.

1. Fix me for _ my star - ry crown.
2. Fix me for _ my dy - ing bed.
Fix me, Je - sus, fix me.

Words: Traditional
Music: Negro Spiritual; arr. Verolga Nix (b. 1933)
Arr. Copyright © 1981 Abingdon. Reprinted from *Songs of Zion* by permission.

Here Am I, Send Me

1. Hark! the voice of Je - sus call - ing, Who will
2. Let none hear you i - dly say - ing, There is
3. Take the task He gives you glad - ly, Let His

1. go and work to - day? Fields are ripe the har - vest
2. noth - ing I can do; While the souls of some are
3. work your pleas - ure be; An - swer quick - ly when He

1. wait - ing, Who will bear the sheaves a - way?
2. dy - ing, And the Mas - ter calls for you.
3. call - eth, "Here am I, send me, send me."

Loud and long the Mas - ter call - eth, Rich re - ward He of - fers free;

Who will an - swer, glad - ly say - ing. "Here am I, send me, send me."

Words: Daniel March
Music: J.C. Lenderman

127

His Name So Sweet

Oh Lord, I jes' come from de foun-tain, I'm jus' from de foun-tain, Lord, _ I

jes' come from de foun-tain His Name so sweet. Oh Lord, I

Fine

Name so sweet. 1. Po' sin-ner, do you love Je-sus? Yes, yes, I
2. Class lead-er, do you love Je-sus?
3. Zidh' El-der, do you love Je-sus?

D.S.

1.Sin-ner, do you love Je-sus?
do love my Je-sus. 2.Lead-er, do you love Je-sus? His name so sweet. Oh Lord, I
3.El-der, do you love Je-sus?

Words: Traditional
Music: Negro Spiritual; arr. Hall Johnson (1888-1970), from *30 Negro Spirituals for Voice & Piano*
Arr. Copyright © 1949 (Renewed) G. Schirmer, Inc. International Copyright Secured. All Rights Reserved.
Used by Permission.

2. Sounds like Jesus. Somebody's callin' mah name, ...
3. Soon one mornin', death'll come creepin' in mah room, ...
4. I'm so glad. Ah got my religion in time, ...
5. I'm so glad. I'm on my journey home, ...

Words: Traditional
Music: Negro Spiritual; arr. Moses Hogan. Used by Permission.

I Am Thine, O Lord

1. I am thine, O Lord, I have heard thy voice, And it
2. Con - se - crate me now to thy ser - vice, Lord, By the
3. Oh, the pure de - light of a sin - gle hour That be -
4. There are depths of love that I can - not know Till I

1. told thy love to me; But I long to rise in the
2. pow'r of grace di - vine; Let my soul look up with a
3. fore thy throne I spend, When I kneel in prayer, and with
4. cross the nar - row sea; There are heights of joy that I

1. arms of faith, And be clos - er drawn to thee.
2. stead - fast hope, And my will be lost in thine.
3. thee, my God, I com - mune as friend with friend!
4. may not reach Till I rest in peace with thee.

Draw me near - er, near-er, bless-ed Lord, To the

near - er, near - er,

cross where thou has died, Draw me near - er, near - er,

Words: Fanny J. Crosby (1820-1915)
Music: William H. Doane (1832-1915)

near - er, bless - ed Lord, To thy pre - cious, bleed - ing side.

Glory, Glory, Hallelujah 130

1. Glo - ry, glo - ry, _____ hal - le - lu - jah! _____
2. I feel bet - ter, _____ so much bet - ter, _____

1. _____ Since I laid my _____ bur - den down, _____
2. _____ Since I laid my _____ bur - den down, _____

1. _____ Glo - ry, glo - ry, _____ hal - le - lu - jah! _____
2. _____ I feel bet - ter, _____ so much _ bet - ter, _____

1. _____ Since I laid my _____ bur - den down.
2. _____ Since I laid my _____ bur - den down. _____

3. Feel like shouting, "Hallelujah!" etc.
4. I am climbing Jacobs ladder. etc.

Words: Traditional
Music: Negro Spiritual; arr. Carl Haywood (b. 1949), from *The Haywood Collection of Negro Spirituals*,
Copyright © 1992.

I Know the Lord's Laid His Hands on Me

O I know the Lord, _____ I know the Lord, _____
I know the Lord's _ laid His hands on me, O hands on me.

1. Did ev - er you _ see the like be - fore _____
   Je - sus _ preach - ing to the poor? _____
2. O was - n't _ that a hap - py day _____
   Je - sus _ washed my sins a - way? _____
3. Some _ seek the Lord and don't seek Him _ right.
   fool _ all _ day and pray at night. _____
4. My _ Lord's _ done just what He said, _____
   healed _ the _ sick and raised the dead. _____

Words: Traditional
Music: Negro Spiritual; arr R. Nathaniel Dett (1882-1943)

1. I know the Lord's _ laid His hands on me, King hands on me.
2. I know the Lord's _ laid His hands on me, When hands on me.
3. I know the Lord's _ laid His hands on me, They hands on me.
4. I know the Lord's _ laid His hands on me, He's hands on me.

Cert'nly, Lord

132

1. Have you got good re-li-gion? Cer-t'nly, Lord! _ Have you got good re-li-gion? Cer-t'nly, Lord! _ Have you got good re-li-gion? Cer-t'nly, Lord! _____ Cer-t'nly, cer-t'nly, cer-t'nly, Lord! _

2. Have you been redeemed?   Cert'nly, Lord!
3. Have you been to the water?   Cert'nly, Lord!
4. Have you been baptized?   Cert'nly, Lord!

Words: Traditional
Music: Negro Spiritual

I Surrender All

1. All to Je - sus I sur - ren - der,
   I will ev - er love and trust Him,
2. All to Je - sus I sur - ren - der
   World - ly pleas - ures all for - sak - en,
3. All to Je - sus I sur - ren - der
   Let me feel the Ho - ly Spir - it
4. All to Je - sus I sur - ren - der
   Fill me with thy love and pow - er,

1. All to Him I free - ly give;
   In His pres - ence dai - ly live.
2. Hum - bly at His feet I bow;
   Take me, Je - sus, take me now.
3. Make me, Sav - ior, whol - ly thine;
   Tru - ly know that thou art mine.
4. Lord, I give my - self to thee;
   Let thy bless - ings fall on me.

I sur - ren - der all,
I sur - ren - der all,
I sur - ren - der all,
I sur - ren - der all.
All to thee, my

Words: Judson W. Van de Vanter (1855-1939)
Music: Winfield S. Weeden (1847-1908)

bless - ed Sav - ior, I sur - ren - der all.

Take Me to the Water

1. Take me to the wa - - - ter, take me to the
2. None __ but the right - - eous, none __ but the
3. I __ love __ Je - - sus, I __ love __
4. He's __ my __ Sav - - ior, He's __ my __

1. wa - - fer, __ take me to the wa - - -
2. right - - eous, __ none __ but the right - - -
3. Je - - sus, __ I __ love __ Je - - -
4. Sav - - ior, __ He's __ my __ Sav - - -

1. ter to be bap - tized.
2. eous. __ shall see God.
3. sus, oh yes, I do.
4. ior, oh yes, He is.

Words: Traditional
Music: Negro Spiritual; arr. Horace Clarence Boyer (b. 1935)
Arr. Copyright © 1992 Horace Clarence Boyer

Is Your All on the Altar

1. You have longed for sweet peace and for faith to in-
2. Would you walk with the Lord in the light of His
3. O we nev - er can know what the Lord will be-
4. Who can tell all the love He will send from a-

1. crease, And have ear - nest-ly, fer - vent-ly prayed; _____
2. word, And have peace and con - tent - ment al - way? _____
3. stow Of the bless - ings for which we have prayed _____
4. bove, And how hap - py our hearts will be made; _____

1. But you can - not have rest or be per - fect-ly blest
2. You must do His sweet will to be free from all ill,
3. Till our bod - y and soul He doth ful - ly con - trol,
4. Of the char - i - ty sweet we shall share at His feet

1. Un - til all on the al - tar is laid. _____
2. On the al - tar your all you must lay. _____
3. And our all on the al - tar is laid. _____
4. When our all on the al - tar is laid. _____

Words: Elisha A. Hoffman (1839-1929)
Music: Elisha A. Hoffman

Is your all on the al - tar of sac - ri - fice laid?

Your heart does the Spir - it con - trol? _____

You can on - ly be blest and have peace and sweet rest

As you yield Him your bod - y and soul. _____

I Have Decided to Follow Jesus

1. I have decided to follow Jesus,
2. Though no one join me, still I will follow,
3. The world behind me, the cross before me,

1. I have decided to follow Jesus,
2. Though no one join me, still I will follow,
3. The world behind me, the cross before me,

1. I have decided to follow Jesus,
2. Though no one join me, still I will follow,
3. The world behind me, the cross before me,

No turning back, no turning back!
(no turning back,)

Words: Ascribed to an Indian Prince; as sung in Garo, Assam
Music: Indian Folk Melody; arr. Norman Johnson

Just As I Am

Words: Charlotte Elliott (1789-1871)
Music: William B. Bradbury (1816-1868)

1. Lord, I want to be a Chris-tian In my heart, In my heart; —
2. Lord, I want to be more lov-ing In my heart, In my heart; —
3. Lord, I want to be more ho-ly In my heart, In my heart; —
4. I don't want to be like Ju-das In my heart, In my heart; —
5. Lord, I want to be like Je-sus In my heart, In my heart; —

1. Lord, I want to be a Chris-tian In my heart,_____
2. Lord, I want to be more lov-ing In my heart,_____
3. Lord, I want to be more ho-ly In my heart,_____
4. I don't want to be like Ju-das In my heart,_____
5. Lord, I want to be like Je-sus In my heart,_____

In my heart,_____ In my heart,_____
In my heart,   In my heart,

1. Lord, I want to be a Chris-tian In my heart._____
2. Lord, I want to be more lov-ing In my heart._____
3. Lord, I want to be more ho-ly In my heart._____
4. I don't want to be like Ju-das In my heart._____
5. Lord, I want to be like Je-sus In my heart._____

Words: Traditional
Music: Negro Spiritual; arr. Edward C. Deas

1. Pass me not, O gentle Savior, Hear my humble cry;
2. Let me at thy throne of mercy Find a sweet relief;
3. Trusting only in thy merit, Would I seek thy face;
4. Thou the spring of all my comfort, More than life to me,

1. While on others thou art calling, Do not pass me by.
2. Kneeling there in deep contrition, Help my unbelief.
3. Heal my wounded, broken spirit, Save me by thy grace.
4. Whom have I on earth beside thee? Whom in heav'n but thee?

Savior, Savior, Hear my humble cry;

While on others thou art calling, Do not pass me by.

Words: Fanny J. Crosby (1820-1915)
Music: William H. Doane (1832-1915)

Lord, I Want You To Touch Me

Lord, I want you to touch me, _____ Touch me with
Thy ho - ly love. _____ Lord, come down and
touch me. _____ Come down from heav - en a - bove. _____
Lord, reach out and touch me, _____
Reach out and touch me with - in, _____ Lord,

Words: Martha E. Banks
Music: Martha E. Banks; harm. James A. Jones; special harm. Clara Ward (1924-1973)
Harm. Used by Permission. E PUB 94661

Shall We Gather at the River

1. Shall we gath-er at the riv - er, Where bright an-gel feet have trod;___
2. On the mar-gin of the riv - er, Wash-ing up its sil-ver spray,___
3. Ere we reach the shin-ing riv - er, Lay we ev-'ry bur-den down;___
4. Soon we'll reach the shin-ing riv - er, Soon our pil-grim-age will cease,___

1. With its crys-tal tide for-ev - er Flow-ing by the_ throne of _ God?
2. We will walk and wor-ship ev - er, All the hap-py_ gold-en _ day.
3. Grace our spir-its will de-liv - er, And pro-vide a _ robe and _ crown.
4. Soon our hap-py hearts will quiv - er With the mel-o - dy of _ peace.

Yes, we'll gath-er at the riv - er, The beau-ti-ful, the beau-ti-ful_ riv - er;

Gath-er with the saints _ at the riv - er That flows by the throne of _ God.

Words: Robert Lowry (1826-1899)
Music: Robert Lowry

Wade in the Water

Words: Traditional
Music: Negro Spiritual; arr. Carl Haywood (b. 1949), from *The Haywood Collection of Negro Spirituals*, Copyright © 1992.

Where He Leads Me

144

1. I can hear my Sav - ior call - ing, __ I can hear my Sav ior call - ing, __
2. I'll go with Him through the gar - den, __ I'll go with Him through the gar - den, __
3. I'll go with Him through the judge- ment, __ I'll go with Him through the judge- ment, __
4. He will give me grace and glo - ry, __ He will give me grace and glo - ry, __

1. I can hear my Sav - ior call - ing, _ "Take thy cross and fol- low, fol- low me."
2. I'll go with Him through the gar - den, _ I'll go with Him, with Him, all the way.
3. I'll go with Him through the judge- ment, _ I'll go with Him, with Him all the way.
4. He will give me grace and glo - ry, __ And go with me, with me all the way.

Where He leads me I will fol- low, __ Where He leads me I will fol- low, __

Where He leads me I will fol- low, __ I'll go with Him, with Him all the way.

Words: E. W. Blandy, c. 1890
Music: John S. Norris (1844-1907)

Have Thine Own Way, Lord!

1. Have thine own way, Lord! Have thine own way! ___
2. Have thine own way, Lord! Have thine own way! ___
3. Have thine own way, Lord! Have thine own way! ___
4. Have thine own way, Lord! Have thine own way! ___

1. Thou art the pot - ter, I am the clay! ___
2. Search me and try me, Mas - ter, to - day! ___
3. Wound - ed and wea - ry, Help me, I pray! ___
4. Hold o'er my be - ing Ab - so - lute sway! ___

1. Mold me and make me Aft - er thy will, ___
2. Pur - er than snow, Lord, Wash me just now, ___
3. Pow - er all pow - er Sure - ly is thine! ___
4. Fill with thy Spir - it 'Til all shall see ___

1. While I am wait - ing, Yield - ed and still. ___
2. As in thy pres - ence Hum - bly I bow. ___
3. Touch me and heal me, Sav - ior di - vine! ___
4. Christ on - ly, al - ways, Liv - ing in me! ___

Words: Adelaide A. Pollard (1862-1934)
Music: George C. Stebbins (1846-1945)

COMMUNION

Break Thou the Bread of Life 146

1. Break thou the bread of life, Dear Lord, to me,
2. Bless thou the truth, dear Lord, To me, to me,
3. Teach me to live, dear Lord, On - ly for thee,

1. As thou didst break the loaves Be - side the sea;
2. As thou didst bless the bread By Gal - i - lee;
3. As thy dis - ci - ples lived in Gal - i - lee;

1. Be - yond the sa - cred page I seek thee, Lord;
2. Then shall all bond - age cease, All fet - ters fall,
3. Then, all my strug - gles o'er, Then, vic - t'ry won,

1. My spir - it pants for thee, O liv - ing word!
2. And I shall find my peace, My all in all.
3. I shall be - hold thee, Lord, The liv - ing one.

Words: Mary A. Lathbury (1841-1913)
Music: William F. Sherwin (1826-1888)

147   **Come, ye Disconsolate**

1. Come, ye dis - con - so - late, wher - e'er ye lan - guish,
2. Joy of the des - o - late, light___ of the stray - ing,
3. Here see the bread of life; see___ wa - ters flow - ing

1. Come to the mer - cy - seat, fer - vent - ly kneel:
2. Hope of the pen - i - tent, fade - less and pure!
3. Forth from the throne of God, pure from a - bove:

1. Here bring your wound - ed hearts, here tell__ your__ an - guish;
2. Here speaks the com - fort - er, ten - der - ly__ say - ing,
3. Come to the feast of love; come, ev - er__ know - ing

1. Earth __ has no sor - row that heav'n can - not heal.
2. "Earth __ has no sor - row that heav'n can - not cure."
3. Earth __ has no sor - row but heav'n can re - move.

Words: Stanzas 1-2, Thomas Moore (1779-1852); Stanza 3, Thomas Hasting (1784-1872)
Music: Sammuel Webbe (1740-1816)

Words: Traditional
Music: Negro Spiritual; arr. Carl Diton (1886-1969), from *36 South Carolina Spirituals*
Arr. Copyright © 1930 (Renewed) G. Schirmer, Inc. International Copyright Secured. All Rights Reserved.
Used by Permission.

In Remembrance of Me

1. In re - mem - brance of me,
2. (In re -) mem - brance of me,

1. eat this bread. ___ In re - mem - brance of me, drink this wine. ___ In re -
2. heal the sick. ___ In re - mem - brance of me, feed the poor. ___ In re -

1. mem - brance of me, pray for the time when God's ___ own will is
2. mem - brance of me, o - pen the door and let ___ your broth - er

1.
done. ___ In re -

2.
in, Let ___ him in. ___

Take, eat, and be com - fort - ed; drink and re - mem - ber

Words: Ragan Courtney
Music: Buryl Red; arr. Robert F. Douglas

Jesus, the Bread of Life

Je - sus, the Bread of life, Je -

sus, the Bread of life. All who eat and

drink of Him will nev - er die, _____

Fine

_____ will nev - er die. _____

Fine

1. I am the Bread that came down from heav - en.
2. All who come to me will not hun - ger,
3. All who love and keep my com - mand - ments

One Bread, One Body

One bread, ___ one bod-y, ___

one Lord of all, _____ one cup of

bless - ing which we bless. _____ And we, ___ though

man- y, _____ through - out the earth, we are one

Last time

bod - y in this one _____ Lord. _____

Last time

1. Gen - tile   or   Jew,   ser - vant   or
2. Man - y   the   gifts,   man - y   the
3. Grain for   the   fields,   scat - tered   and

1. free, wom-an or man, _____
2. works, one in the Lord _____
3. grown, gath-ered to one _____

D.S.

1. __ no more. _____ One
2. __ of all. _____ One
3. __ for all. _____ One

D.S.

✠ **CODA**

Lord. _____

Let Us Break Bread Together

1. Let us break bread to-geth-er on our knees (on our
2. Let us drink wine to-geth-er on our knees (on our

1. knees); Let us break bread to-geth-er on our knees (on our
2. knees); Let us drink wine to-geth-er on our knees (on our

1. knees).
2. knees). When I fall on my knees, with my face to the ris - ing

sun, Oh __ Lord, have mer-cy on me (on me). me).

Let us praise God to-geth-er on our knees (yes, on our knees); Let us

praise God to-geth-er on our knees (yes on our knees). When I

fall on my knees, with my face to the ris-ing sun, Oh ___

Lord, have mer-cy on me (on me).

Lord I Have Seen Thy Salvation

1. Lord I have seen thy sal-va-tion, _____ Lord I have seen thy sal-
2. Lord I have heard of thy king-dom, _____ Lord I have heard of thy

1. va-tion, __ drank of the blood, held the
2. pro-mise, __ looked on thy birth, cried at

1. bo-dy, _____ Lord I have seen, seen with my eyes, seen with my
2. Cal-v'ry, _____ Lord I have heard, Lord I have heard, Lord I have

Words: John D. Cooper (b. 1925)
Music: John D. Cooper
Copyright © 1980 Dangerfield Music Co., 286 Strawberry Hill Rd., Centerville, MA.

1. heart.
2. heard.

Fell on my knees, down at the al-tar,— bowed down my head, whisp-ered a pray-er._____ Have mer-cy Lord, I'm not wor-thy,_____ I ___ be-lieve, Yes, I be-lieve, now I am sure.

Taste and See

Taste and see. Taste and see the good - ness

of the Lord. O Taste and see. Taste and

Fine

see the good - ness of the Lord, of the Lord.

1. I will bless the Lord at all times.
2. Glo - ri - fy the Lord with me.
3. Wor - ship the Lord all you peo - ple.

Words: Psalm 34
Music: James E. Moore, Jr.

1. His praise shall al-ways be on my
2. To - geth - er let us all praise His
3. You'll want for noth - ing if you

1. lips; my soul shall
2. name. I called the
3. ask. Taste and

1. glo - ry in the Lord; for
2. Lord and He ans - swered me; from
3. see that God is good; in

D.C.

1. He has been so good to me.
2. all my trou - bles He set me free.
3. Him we need put all our trust.

This Is My Body

This is my bod - y __ giv-en up for you, _____ this is my

blood ____ poured out for you. _____ This is my bod - y __ giv - en

up for you, _____ this is my blood ____ poured out for you. _____

Words: From *Mary, Cause of Our Joy*
Music: Edward V. Bonnemere

Bod-y of Christ, A - men, _____ Blood of

Christ, A - men, _____ Bod-y of Christ.

A - men, _____ Blood of Christ, A - men. _____

EVANGELISM

156

Come to Me

1. "Come to me, Ye who are hard ___ op - pressed;
2. "Come to me!" Je - ho - vah gen - tly pleads;

1. Lay your head gen - tly up - on ___ my breast; ___
2. "Come to me, I can sup - ply ___ all needs; ___

1. Come to me, And I will give ___ you rest; wea - ry
2. And my way, Un - to green pas - ture leads; Free from

1. one, Hith - er come! God is your home!"
2. sin! En - ter in! God is your home!"

Words: Traditional
Music: Negro Spiritual; arr. R. Nathaniel Dett (1882-1943)

1. We praise thee, O God, For the son of thy love, For Jesus who died And is now gone above.
2. We praise thee, O God, For thy spirit of light, Who has shown us our Savior, And scattered our night.
3. All glory and praise To the lamb that was slain, Who has borne all our sins And has cleansed ev'ry stain.
4. Revive us again, Fill each heart with thy love, May each soul be rekindled With fire from above.

Refrain: Hallelujah! Thine the glory, Hallelujah! Amen, Hallelujah! Thine the glory, Revive us again.

Words: William P. MacKay (1837-1885)
Music: John H. Husband (1760-1825)

Make Me a Blessing

1. Out in the high - ways and by - ways of life, _____
2. Tell the sweet sto - ry of Christ and His love, _____
3. Give as 'twas giv - en to you in your need, _____

1. Man - y are wea - ry and sad; _____
2. Tell of His power to for - give; _____
3. Love as the Mas - ter loved you; _____

1. Car - ry the sun - shine where dark - ness is rife,
2. Oth - ers will trust Him if on - ly you prove
3. Be to the help - less a help - er in - deed,

1. Mak - ing the sor - row - ing glad. _____
2. True, ev - ery mo - ment you live. _____
3. Un - to your mis - sion be true. _____

Words: Ira B. Wilson (1880-1950)
Music: George Schuler (1882-1973)

Lift Him Up

1. How to reach the mass-es, those of ev-'ry birth, For an
2. Oh! the world is hun-gry for the liv-ing bread, Lift the
3. Don't ex-alt the preach-er, don't ex-alt the pew, Preach the
4. Lift Him up by liv-ing as a chris-tian ought, Let the

1. an-swer Je-sus gave the key; "And__ I, if I be lift-ed
2. Sav-ior up for them to see; Trust__ Him and do not doubt the
3. gos-pel sim-ple, full and free; Prove__ Him and you will find that
4. world in you the Sav-ior see; Then__ all will glad-ly fol-low

1. up from the earth, Will draw all men* un-to Me."
2. words that He said, "I'll draw all men* un-to Me."
3. prom-ise is true, "I'll draw all men* un-to Me."
4. Him who once taught, "I'll draw all men* un-to Me."

Lift Him up, _____ Lift Him up, _____

Lift the pre-cious sav-ior up, Lift the pre-cious sav-ior up,

Still He speaks from e-ter-ni-ty: "And__ I, if I be lift-ed

Words: Johnson Oatman, Jr. (1856-1922)
Music: B. B. Beall

up   from   the   earth,   Will   draw   all   men*   un - to   Me."

* "folk" may be substituted for "men."

This Little Light of Mine 160

1. This lit - tle light of mine, ___ I'm goin' - a let it shine, ___

this lit - tle light of mine, ___ I'm goin' - a let it shine, ___

this lit - tle light of mine, ___ I'm goin' - a let it shine,

let it shine, let it shine, let it shine (let it shine).

2. Everywhere I go...   3. All through the night...

Words: Traditional
Music: Negro Spiritual; adapt. William Farley Smith (b. 1941)
Adapt. Copyright © 1989 The United Methodist Publishing House. Reprinted from *The United Methodist Hymnal* by permission.

Go Preach My Gospel

1. "Go____ preach my gos - pel," saith the Lord, "Bid__
2. "I'll____ make my great____ com - mis - sion known, And__
3. "Go____ heal the sick,____ go raise the dead, Go__
4. "While__ thus ye fol - low my com- mands, I'm__
5. He____ spake and light____ shone round His head, On__

1. the whole earth__ my grace re - ceive, Ex - plain to them my
2. ye shall prove__ my gos - pel true By all the works that
3. cast out dev - ils in my name. Nor let my proph - ets
4. with you till____ the world shall end. All pow'r in trust - ed
5. a bright cloud__ to heav'n He rode. They to the far - thest

1. sa - cred word, Bid____ them be - lieve,__ o - bey, and live."____
2. I have done, And____ all the won - ders ye shall do."____
3. be a - fraid, Though__ man re - proach,__ and will blas - pheme."__
4. in my hands; I____ can de - stroy,__ and can de - fend."____
5. na - tion spread The____ grace of their__ as - cend - ed God.____

Words: Isaac Watts (1674-1748)
Music: Thomas Hastings (1784-1872)

PRAYER

Come by Here *(Kum bah-ya)* 162

1. Come by here Lord, come by here,
Come by here Lord, come by here, Come by here Lord,
come by here, O Lord, come by here.

2. Someone needs you Lord, come by here.

3. Send a blessing Lord, come by here.

Words: Traditional
Music: Negro Spiritual; arr. Richard Smallwood
Arr. used by permission of Century Oak/Richwood Music.

Come Here Jesus, If You Please

No harm have I done you on my knees, (on my knees,) No harm have I done you on my knees, (on my knees,) When you see me on my knees, dear Lord, come here, Je - sus, if you please.

A - men, A - men, A - men, A - men, A - - - men.

please.

Words: Roland M. Carter (b. 1942)
Music: Roland M. Carter
Copyright © Mar-Vel, Chattanooga, TN 37401.

1. Do   Lord,____ do Lord, Do re - mem - ber me,
2. When I'm   in   trou - ble, Do re - mem - ber me,
3. When I'm____ dy - in', Do re - mem - ber me,
4. When this world's on fire, Do re - mem - ber me,

1. Do   Lord,____ do Lord, Do re - mem - ber me,____
2. When I'm   in   trou - ble, Do re - mem - ber me,____
3. When I'm____ dy - in', Do re - mem - ber me,____
4. When this world's on fire, Do re - mem - ber me,____

1. Do   Lord,____ do Lord, Do re - mem - ber me,
2. When I'm   in   trou - ble, Do re - mem - ber me,
3. When I'm____ dy - in', Do re - mem - ber me,
4. When this world's on fire, Do re - mem - ber me,

O

Do Lord re - mem - ber me.

Words: Traditional
Music: Negro Spiritual; arr. John W. Work (1901-1967). Used by permission of Mrs. J. W. Work.

1. I'm press-ing on the up-ward way, New heights I'm
2. My heart has no de-sire to stay Where doubts a-
3. I want to live a-bove the world, Though sa-tan's
4. I want to scale the ut-most height, And catch a

1. gain - ing ev-ery day; Still pray-ing as I on-ward bound,
2. rise and fears dis-may; Though some may dwell where these a-bound,
3. darts at me are hurled; For faith has caught a joy-ful sound,
4. gleam of glo-ry bright; But still I'll pray till heav'n I've found,

1. "Lord, plant my feet on high - er ground."
2. My prayer, my aim is high - er ground. Lord, lift me
3. The song of saints on high - er ground.
4. "Lord, lead me on to high - er ground."

up, and let me stand By faith, on heav - en's ta-ble-land; A high-er

plane than I have found, Lord, plant my feet on high - er ground.

Words: Johnson Oatman, Jr. (1860-1948)
Music: Charles H. Gabriel (1856-1932)

Grant Me a Blessing

Hymn continues on the next page.

Words: Joseph N. Heard
Music: Joseph N. Heard

Grant __ me a bless - ing, Grant __ me a bless - ing,

Grant __ me a bless-ing, A bless-ing to - day, _____ to - day.

167

Even Me

1. Lord I hear of show'rs of bless - ings, _____
2. Pass me not, O gen - tle Sav - ior, _____
3. Bread of heav - en, bread of heav - en, _____
4. Love of God, so pure and change - less, _____

1. Thou are scat - t'ring full and free; _____
2. Sin - ful though my heart may be; _____
3. Ev - er let me feed on thee; _____
4. Blood of Christ, so rich, so free; _____

Words: Traditional
Music: Negro Spiritual; harm. Roberta Martin (1912-1969)

1. Show'rs the thirst - y souls re - fresh - ing, _____
2. I am long - ing for thy fa - vor, _____
3. Vine of heav - en, vine of heav - en, _____
4. Grace of God, so strong and bound - less, _____

1. Let some drops now fall on me!
2. Whilst thou'rt bless - ing, Oh bless me!
3. Let thy blood a - tone for me!
4. Mag - ni - fy them all in me!

E - ven me, yes! E - ven me! _____

E - ven me, Lord! E - ven me! _____

1. Let some drops now fall ___ on me! _____
2. Whilst thou'rt bless - ing, Lord, ___ bless me! _____
3. Let thy blood a - tone ___ for me! _____
4. Mag - ni - fy them all ___ in me! _____

I Am Praying for You

1. I have a Savior, He's pleading in glory,
2. I have a Father, to me He has given
3. I have a robe: 'tis resplendent in whiteness,
4. When Jesus has found you, tell others the story,

1. A dear, loving savior, though earth-friends be few;
2. A hope for eternity, blessed and true;
3. A-waiting in glory my wondering view;
4. That my loving savior is your savior, too;

1. And now He is watching in tenderness o'er me,
2. And soon will He call me to meet Him in heaven,
3. Oh, when I receive it all shining in brightness,
4. Then pray that your Savior may bring them to glory,

1. And, oh, that my Savior were your savior, too.
2. But, oh, that He'd let me bring you with me, too!
3. Dear friend, could I see you receiving one, too!
4. And prayer will be answered, 'twas answered for you!

Words: S. O'Malley Cluff
Music: Ira D. Sankey (1840-1908)

Sometimes I Feel Like a Motherless Chile

169

Hymn continues on the next page.

Words: Traditional
Music: Negro Spiritual; arr. Carl Haywood (b. 1949), from *The Haywood Collection of Negro Spirituals*,
Copyright © 1992.

long ways __ from home, _____ A long

ways _ from home. _____ Then I get down on my knees _ an'

pray, _____ Get down on my knees _ an' pray.

170   **Yield Not to Temptation**

1. Yield not to temp-ta - tion, For yield-ing is sin; ____
2. Shun e - vil com-pan - ions, Bad lan-guage dis - dain; ___
3. To him that o'er-com - eth, God giv-eth a crown; __

Words: Horatio R. Palmer (1834-1907)
Music: Horatio R. Palmer; arr. Carl Haywood (b. 1949), from *Songs of Praise*, Harm. Copyright © 1992.

1. Each vic-t'ry will help you, Some o-ther to win; ___
2. God's name hold in rev - 'rence, Nor take it in vain; ___
3. Through faith we will con - quer, Though oft-en cast down; ___

1. Fight, still pres-sing on - ward, Dark pas-sions sub - due; ___
2. Be thought-ful and ear - nest, Kind - heart-ed and true; ___
3. He who is our sav - ior, Our strength will re - new; ___

Look ev - er to Je - sus, He will car - ry you through. _

Ask the sav - ior to help you, Com - fort, strength-en and keep you;

He is will - ing to aid you, He will car - ry you through. _

I Couldn't Hear Nobody Pray

Words: Traditional
Music: Negro Spiritual; arr. Carl Haywood (b. 1949), from *The Haywood Collection of Negro Spirituals*,
Copyright © 1992.

1. On ma knees, ____   Wid ma bur-den, ___
2. In de Jer-den, ___   Cross-in' o - ver, ___
3. Trou-bles o - ver ___   In de king-dom, ___

pray,   Could-n't hear no-bod-y pray,   Could-n't hear no-bod-y

D.S.

1. An' ma Sav - ior. ____   O ma Lord, ___
2. In - to Ca - naan. ___
3. Wid my Je - sus. ____

D.S.

pray,   Could-n't hear no-bod - y pray,   I

No - bod - y knows the trou - ble I see, Lord,

No - bod - y knows the trou - ble I see; No - bod - y knows the

Fine

trou - ble I see, Lord, ___ No - bod - y knows but Je - sus.

Broth - er, will you pray for me? Broth - er, will you pray for me?

D.C.

Broth - er, will you pray for me, And help me to drive old sa - tan a - way?

Words: Traditional
Music: Negro Spiritual; arr. R. Nathaniel Dett (1882-1943)

2. Sister, will you pray for me?
   Sister, will you pray for me?
   Sister, will you pray for me,
   And help me to drive old satan away?

3. Father, will you pray for me?
   Father, will you pray for me?
   Father, will you pray for me,
   And help me to drive old satan away?

4. Mother, will you pray for me?
   Mother, will you pray for me?
   Mother, will you pray for me,
   And help me to drive old satan away?

Keep Me Every Day 173

1. Lord, I want to live __ for thee, Ev - 'ry day __ and hour;
2. In my weak-ness be __ my strength; In my tri - als all,
3. Leave me not to walk __ a - lone, Lest I droop __ and die;

1. Let thy spi - rit be __ with me, In its sav - ing pow'r!
2. Be thou near me all __ the day, Hear my ev - 'ry call!
3. Let thy spir - it go __ with me, And at - tend __ my cry!

Keep my heart, and keep my hand, Keep my soul, I pray!

Keep my tongue to speak __ thy praise, Keep me all __ the way!

Words: F. L. Eiland
Music: Emmet S. Dean

174   **Let the Heav'n Light Shine on Me**

Words: Roland M. Carter (b. 1942)
Music: Roland M. Carter
Copyright © Mar-Vel. Chattanooga, TN 37401.

Words: Traditional
Music: Negro Spiritual

An Evening Prayer

1. If   I   have wound-ed an - y soul   to - day,
2. If   I   have ut - tered i - dle words   or   vain,
3. If   I   have been per - verse, or   hard,   or   cold,
4. For - give   the sins   I   have con - fessed   to   thee;

1. If   I   have caused one   foot   to   go   a - stray,
2. If   I   have turned a - side from   want   or   pain,
3. If   I   have longed for   shel - ter   in   the   fold,
4. For - give   the se - cret sins   I   do   not   see;

1. If   I   have walked in   my   own   will - ful   way,
2. Lest   I   of - fend some oth - er   through   the   strain,
3. When   thou   hast giv - en   me   some   fort   to   hold,
4. O   guide   me, love me, and   my   keep - er   be.

1.2.3.   D.C.   4.

Dear_ Lord,_ for - give (for - give)!   A - men (A - men).

Words: C. M. Battersby
Music: Charles Gabriel (1856-1932)

Words: Traditional
Music: Negro Spiritual; arr. Carl Haywood (b. 1949), from *The Haywood Collection of Negro Spirituals*,
Copyright © 1992.

1. Sweet hour of prayer, sweet hour of prayer, That calls me from a
2. Sweet hour of prayer, sweet hour of prayer, Thy wings shall my pe-
3. Sweet hour of prayer, sweet hour of prayer, May I thy con - so-

1. world of care, And bids me at my Fa - ther's throne Make
2. ti - tion bear To Him whose truth and faith - ful - ness En-
3. la - tion share, Till from Mount Pis - gah's loft - y height I

1. all my wants and wish - es known. In sea - sons of dis-
2. gage the wait - ing soul to bless; And since He bids me
3. view my home and take my flight: This robe of flesh I'll

1. tress and grief My soul has of - ten found re - lief.
2. seek His face, Be - lieve His word and trust His grace.
3. drop, and rise To seize the ev - er - last - ing prize.

Words: William Walford (1772-1850)
Music: William B. Bradbury (1816-1868)

1. And oft es - caped the tempt - er's snare By
2. I'll cast on Him my ev - 'ry care, And
3. And shout, while pass - ing through the air, "Fare -

1. thy re - turn, sweet hour of prayer.
2. wait for thee, sweet hour of prayer.
3. well, fare - well, sweet hour of prayer!"

Remember Me 179

Re - mem - ber me, Re - mem - ber ___
me, O Lord, re - mem - ber me. ___

Words: Traditional
Music: Negro Spiritual; harm. J. Jefferson Cleveland (1937-1988)
Harm. Copyright © 1981 Abingdon. Reprinted from *Songs of Zion* by permission.

ASSURANCE

Ain'-a That Good News

2. I got a crown up in-a that kingdom.

3. I got a savior in-a that kingdom.

Words: Traditional
Music: Negro Spiritual; arr. Clayton White (b. 1942)
Arr. Copyright © 1978 The Clayton White Singers Choral Series

Amazing Grace

1. A - maz - ing grace! ____ how sweet the sound, That
2. 'Twas grace that taught ____ my heart to fear, And
3. The Lord has prom - ised good to me, His
4. Through man - y dan - gers, toils, and snares, I
5. When we've been there ____ ten thou - sand years, Bright

1. saved a wretch like me! ____ I once was lost, but
2. grace my fears re - lieved; ____ How pre - cious did that
3. word my hope se - cures; ____ He will my shield and
4. have al - read - y come; ____ 'Tis grace that brought me
5. shin - ing as the sun, ____ We've no less days to

1. now am found, Was blind, but now ____ I see. ____
2. grace ap - pear The hour I first ____ be - lieved! ____
3. por - tion be As long as life ____ en - dures. ____
4. safe thus far, And grace will lead ____ me home. ____
5. sing God's praise Than when we'd first ____ be - gun. ____

Words: Stanzas 1-4, John Newton, (1725-1807); Stanza 5, Ascr. John Rees, c. 1859
Music: *New Britain*, CM, *Virginia Harmony*, 1831; harm. John Barnard (b. 1948)
Harm. Copyright © 1982 Hope Publishing Co., Carol Stream, IL 60188. All Rights Reserved. Used by Permission.

Didn't My Lord Deliver Daniel?

Refrain

Did-n't my Lord de-liv-er Dan - iel, ___ de-liv-er Dan - iel, ___ de-liv-er Dan - iel, ___ Did-n't my Lord de-liv-er Dan - iel, ___ An' ___ why not a ev-e-ry man. ___

Fine

Verse 1.

He de-liv-ered Dan-iel from the li-on's den, an' Jo-nah from the bel-ly of the whale; An' the He-brew chil-dren from the fie - ry fur - nace, An' why not ev - e-ry man.

D.C. Refrain

Verse 2.

The win' blows eas' an' de win' blows wes', It

blows like de judg-a-ment __ day; An' ev-ry po' soul __ dat

D.C. Refrain

nev-er did pray 'll be glad to pray __ dat day.

Verse 3.

I set my foot on de gos-pel ship, an' de

ship be-gin __ to __ sail; It land-ed me o-ver on

D.C. al Fine

Ca-naan's shore, __ An' I'll nev-er come back __ no more.

God Will Take Care of You

1. Be not dis-mayed __ what-e'er be-tide, God will take care of you;__
2. Through days of toil __ when heart doth fail, God will take care of you;__
3. All you may need __ He will pro-vide, God will take care of you;__
4. No mat-ter what __ may be the test, God will take care of you;__

1. Be-neath His wings __ of love a-bide, God will take care of you. __
2. When dan-gers fierce __ you path as-sail, God will take care of you. __
3. Noth-ing you ask __ will be de-nied, God will take care of you. __
4. Lean, wea-ry one, __ up-on His breast, God will take care of you. __

God will take care of you, Through ev-'ry day, O'er all the way;

He will take care __ of you, God will take care __ of you. __

Words: Civilla D. Martin (1869-1948)
Music: W. Stillman Martin (1862-1935)

Blessed Assurance

1. Bless-ed as-sur-ance, Je-sus is mine! _____ O what a
2. Per-fect sub-mis-sion, per-fect de-light, _____ Vi-sions of
3. Per-fect sub-mis-sion, all is at rest, _____ I in my

1. fore-taste of glo-ry di-vine! _____ Heir of sal-va-tion, pur-chase of
2. rap-ture now burst on my sight; _____ An-gels de-scend-ing, bring from a-
3. sav-ior am hap-py and blest; _____ Watch-ing and wait-ing, look-ing a-

1. God, _____ Born of His spir-it, washed in His blood. _____
2. bove _____ Ech-oes of mer-cy, whis-pers of love. _____
3. bove, _____ Filled with His good-ness, lost in His love. _____

This is my sto-ry, this is my song, _____ Prais-ing my

Words: Fanny J. Crosby (1820-1915)
Music: Phoebe P. Knapp (1839-1908)

Hymn continues on the next page.

sav - ior all the day long; ___ This is my sto - ry, this is my

song, ___ Prais - ing my sav - ior all the day long. ___

185   **Blessed Quietness**

1. Joys are flow - ing ___ like a riv - er,
2. Bring - ing life and ___ health and glad - ness
3. Like the rain that ___ falls from heav - en,
4. See, a fruit - ful ___ field is grow - ing,
5. What a won - der - ful sal - va - tion,

1. Since the com - fort - er has come; ___
2. All a - round this heav'n - ly guest, ___
3. Like the sun - light from the sky, ___
4. Bless - ed fruit of righ - teous ness; ___
5. When we al - ways see His face, ___

Words: Marie P. Ferguson
Music: W. S. Marshall; arr. J. Jefferson Cleveland (1937-1988) and Verolga Nix (b. 1933)
Arr. Copyright © 1981 Abingdon. Reprinted from *Songs of Zion* by permission.

1. He a - bides with us for - ev - er,
2. Ban - ished un - be - lief and sad - ness,
3. So the Ho - ly Ghost is giv - en,
4. And the streams of life are flow - ing
5. What a per - fect hab - i - ta - tion,

1. Makes the trust - ing heart His home.
2. Chang'd our wea - ri - ness to rest.
3. Com - ing on us from on high.
4. In the lone - ly wil - der - ness.
5. What a qui - et rest - ing place.

Bless-ed qui-et-ness, _ ho - ly qui-et-ness, What as-sur-ance in my soul, _

On the storm-y sea, _ Je-sus speaks to me, And the bil-lows cease to roll. _

Farther Along

1. Tempt - ed and tried we're oft made to won - der, Why it should
2. When death has come and tak - en our loved ones, It leaves our
3. Faith - ful till death said our lov - ing mas - ter, A few more
4. When we see Je - sus com - ing in glo - ry, When He comes

1. be thus all the day long; ____ While there are oth - ers liv - ing a -
2. home so lone - ly and drear; ____ Then do we won - der why oth - ers
3. days to la - bor and wait; ____ Toils of the road will then seem as
4. from His home in the sky; ____ Then we shall meet Him in that bright

1. bout us, Nev - er mo - lest - ed though in the wrong. ____
2. pros - per, Liv - ing so wick - ed year af - ter year. ____
3. noth - ing, As we sweep through the beau - ti - ful gate. ____
4. man - sion, We'll un - der - stand it all by and by. ____

Far - ther a - long we'll know all a - bout it, Far - ther a -

Hymn continues on the next page.

Words: W. B. Stevens
Music: W. B. Stevens; arr. J. R. Baxter, Jr.

long we'll un-der-stand why; ___ Cheer up, don't wor - ry, live in the

sun - shine, We'll un - der - stand it all by and by. ___

188   It Is Well with My Soul

1. When peace, like a riv - er, at - tend - eth my
2. Though sa - tan should buf - fet, though tri - als should
3. My sin— oh, the bliss of this glo - ri - ous
4. And, Lord, haste the day when the faith shall be

1. way, When sor - rows like sea - bil - lows roll;
2. come, Let this blest as - sur - ance con - trol,
3. thought— My sin— not in part, but the whole—
4. sight, The clouds be rolled back as a scroll,

Words: Horatio Spafford (1828-1888)
Music: Philip P. Bliss (1838-1876)

1. What - ev - er my lot, thou hast taught me to
2. That Christ has re - gard - ed my help - less es -
3. Is nailed to the cross and I bear it no
4. The trump shall re - sound and the Lord shall de -

1. say, It is well, it is well with my soul.
2. tate, And has shed His own blood for my soul.
3. more, Praise the Lord, praise the Lord, O my soul!
4. scend, "E - ven so"— it is well with my soul.

It is well _____ with my soul, _____
It is well with my

_____ It is well, it is well with my soul.
soul,

1. Great is thy faith - ful-ness, O God my Fa - ther,
2. Sum - mer and win - ter, and spring - time and har - vest,
3. Par - don for sin and a peace that en - dur - eth,

1. There is no shad - ow of turn - ing with thee;
2. Sun, moon and stars in their cours - es a - bove,
3. Thine own dear pres - ence to cheer and to guide;

1. Thou chang - est not, thy com - pas - sions, they fail not,
2. Join with all na - ture in man - i - fold wit - ness,
3. Strength for to - day and bright hope for to - mor - row,

1. As thou hast been thou for - ev - er wilt be.
2. To thy great faith - ful-ness, mer - cy and love.
3. Bless - ings all mine, with ten thou - sand be - side!

Words: Thomas O. Chisholm (1866-1960)
Music: William M. Runyan (1870-1957)

Great is thy faith - ful- ness! Great is thy faith - ful- ness!

Morn - ing by morn - ing new mer - cies I see;

All I have need - ed thy hand hath pro - vid - ed,

Great is Thy faith - ful- ness, Lord un - to me!

He'll Understand, and Say "Well Done"

1. If ___ when you give ___ the best ___ of your ser-vice, ___
2. Mis - un - der - stood, ___ the sav - ior of sin - ners, ___
3. If ___ when this life ___ of la - bor is end - ed, ___
4. But ___ if you try ___ and fail ___ in your try - ing, ___

1. Tell - ing the world ___ that the Sav - ior has come; ___
2. Hung ___ on the cross; ___ He was God's ___ on - ly Son; ___
3. And ___ the re - ward ___ of the race ___ you have run; ___
4. Hands ___ sore and scarred ___ from the work ___ you've be - gun; ___

1. Be ___ not dis - mayed ___ when friends ___ won't be - lieve you; ___
2. Oh! ___ hear him call ___ His fa - ther in heav - en, ___
3. Oh! ___ the sweet rest ___ pre - pared ___ for the faith - ful, ___
4. Take ___ up your cross, ___ run quick - ly to meet Him, ___

1. He'll ___ un - der - stand, ___ and say ___ "well done." ___
2. "Not ___ my will, ___ but thine ___ be done." ___
3. Will ___ be His blest ___ and fi - nal ___ "well done." ___
4. He'll ___ un - der - stand, ___ and say, ___ "well done." ___

Words: Lucie E. Campbell (1885–1963)
Music: Lucie E. Campbell (1885–1963); arr. Horace Clarence Boyer (b. 1935)

Oh, __ when I come __ to the end __ of my Jour-ney, __

wea - ry of life, __ and the bat - tle is won. __

Car - r'ing the staff __ and the cross __ of re-demp-tion __

He'll __ un - der - stand, __ and say __ "Well done".

His Eye Is on the Sparrow

1. Why should I feel dis-cour-aged, ___ Why should the shad-ows come, ___
2. "Let not your heart be trou-bled," ___ His ten-der word I hear, ___
3. When ev-er I am tempt-ed, ___ When ev-er clouds a-rise, ___

1. Why should my heart be lone-ly, ___ And long for heav'n and home; ___ When
2. And rest-ing on His good-ness, ___ I lose my doubts and fears; ___ Though
3. When songs give place to sigh-ing, ___ When hope with-in me dies, ___ I

1. Je-sus is ___ my por-tion? ___ My con-stant friend ___ is He: ___ His
2. by the path ___ He lead-eth, ___ But one step I ___ may see; ___ His
3. draw the clos-er to Him, ___ From care He sets ___ me free; ___ His

eye is on ___ the spar-row, ___ And I know He watch-es me; ___ His

Words: Civilla D. Martin (1860-1948)
Music: Charles H. Gabriel (1856-1932); arr. Horace Clarence Boyer (b. 1935)
Arr. Copyright © 1992 Horace Clarence Boyer

eye   is   on   the   spar - row, ___   and I know He watch-es   me. ___   I

sing   be - cause I'm hap - py, ___   I   sing   be - cause I'm   free; ___   For His

eye   is   on   the   spar - row, ___   And I know He watch - es   me. ___

I Need Thee Every Hour

1. I need thee ev - 'ry hour, Most gra - cious Lord;
   No ten - der voice like thine Can peace af - ford.
2. I need thee ev - 'ry hour, Stay thou near by;
   Temp - ta - tions lose their power When thou art nigh.
3. I need thee ev - 'ry hour, In joy or pain;
   Come quick - ly and a - bide, Or life is vain.
4. I need thee ev - 'ry hour, Teach me thy will,
   And thy rich prom - is - es In me ful - fill.

I need thee, O I need thee, Ev - 'ry hour I need thee; O
bless me now, my sav - ior, I come to thee.

Words: Annie S. Hawks (1835-1918)
Music: Robert Lowry (1826-1899)

I Will Trust in the Lord

193

1. I __ will __ trust __ in the Lord, __ I will trust ___ in the
2. Sis-ter will you trust __ in the Lord, __ Sis-ter will trust ___ in the

1. Lord, __ I __ will __ trust __ in the Lord 'til I die; _____
2. Lord, __ Sis-ter will you trust __ in the Lord 'til you die; _____

1. __ I __ will __ trust __ in the Lord, I __ will __ trust __ in the
2. __ Sis-ter will you trust __ in the Lord, Sis-ter will you trust __ in the

1. Lord, __ I __ will __ trust __ in the Lord __ 'til I die. _____
2. Lord, __ Sis-ter will you trust __ in the Lord __ 'til you die. _____

3. Brother will you trust in the Lord ('til you die).
4. I'm gonna treat my neighbor right ('til I die).
5. I'm gonna hold my savior's hand ('til I die).

Music: Negro Spiritual; arr. Carl Haywood (b. 1949), from *The Haywood Collection of Negro Spirituals*,
Copyright © 1992.

Lead Me, Guide Me

Lead _ me, guide _ me, a - long the way,
For _____ if you lead me, I can - not stray.
Lord, _____ let me walk each day with Thee.
Lead me, Oh Lord, lead me. _____

Fine

I've Been 'Buked

1. I've been 'buked an' I've been scorned,
2. Dere is trou-ble all o-ver dis worl',
3. Ain' gwine lay my 'li-gion down,

1. I've been 'buked an' I've been scorned, chil - dren;
2. Dere is trou-ble all o-ver dis worl', chil - dren;
3. Ain' gwine lay my 'li-gion down, chil - dren;

1. I've been 'buked an' I've been scourned,
2. Dere is trou-ble all o-ver dis worl',
3. Ain' gwine lay my 'li-gion down,

1. I've been talked a-bout sho's you' born.
2. Dere is trou-ble all o-ver dis worl'.
3. Ain' gwine lay my 'li-gion down.

Words: Traditional
Music: Negro Spiritual; arr. Carl Haywood (b. 1949), from *The Haywood Collection of Negro Spirituals*,
Copyright © 1992.

1. What a fel-low-ship, what a joy di-vine,
2. O how sweet to walk in this pil-grim way,
3. What have I to dread, what have I to fear,

1. Lean-ing on the ev-er-last-ing arms; What a bless-ed-ness,
2. Lean-ing on the ev-er-last-ing arms; O how bright the path
3. Lean-ing on the ev-er-last-ing arms; I have bless-ed peace

1. what a peace is mine, Lean-ing on the ev-er-last-ing arms.
2. grows from day to day, Lean-ing on the ev-er-last-ing arms.
3. with my Lord so near, Lean-ing on the ev-er-last-ing arms.

Lean - ing, lean - ing, safe and se-cure from all a-larms;

Lean-ing on Je-sus, lean-ing on Je-sus,

Lean - ing, lean - ing, Lean-ing on the ev-er-last-ing arms.

Lean-ing on Je-sus, lean-ing on Je-sus

Words: Elisha A. Hoffman (1839-1929)
Music: Anthony J. Showalter (1858-1924); arr. Carl Haywood (b. 1949), from *Songs of Praise*, Copyright © 1992.

197 **Leave It There**

1. If the world from you with-hold, __ of its sil-ver and its gold, __
2. If your bod-y suf-fers pain, __ and your health you can't re-gain, __
3. When your en-e-mies as-sail, __ and your heart be-gins to fail, __
4. When your youth-ful days are gone, __ and old age is steal-ing on. __

1. And you have to get a-long with mea-ger fare; __
2. And your soul is al-most sink-ing in de-spair; __
3. Don't for-get that God in heav-en an-swers prayer; __
4. And your bod-y bends be-neath the weight of care; __

1. Just re-mem-ber in His word. __ How He feeds the lit-tle bird. __
2. Je-sus knows the pain you feel. __ He can save and He can heal. __
3. He will make a way for you, __ and will lead you safe-ly through. __
4. He will nev-er leave you then, __ He'll go with you to the end. __

1. Take your bur-den to the Lord and leave it there. __
2. Take your bur-den to the Lord and leave it there. __
3. Take your bur-den to the Lord and leave it there. __
4. Take your bur-den to the Lord and leave it there. __
(leave it there)

Words: Charles A. Tindley (1851-1933)
Music: Charles A. Tindley; arr. Verolga Nix (b. 1933)

Love Lifted Me

1. I was sink-ing deep in sin, Far from the peace-ful shore, ___
2. All my heart to Him I give, Ev-er to Him I'll cling, ___
3. Souls in dan-ger, look a-bove, Je-sus com-plete-ly saves; ___

1. Ver-y deep-ly stained with-in, Sink-ing to rise no more; ___
2. In His bless-ed pres-ence live, Ev-er His praise-es sing. ___
3. He will lift you by His love Out of the an-gry waves. ___

1. But the mas-ter of the sea Heard my de-spair-ing cry, ___
2. Love so might-y and so true Mer-its my soul's best songs; ___
3. He's the mas-ter of the sea, Bil-lows His will o-bey; ___

1. From the wa-ters lift-ed me— Now safe am I. ___
2. Faith-ful, lov-ing ser-vice, too, To Him be-longs. ___
3. He your sav-ior wants to be— Be saved to-day. ___

Love lift-ed me, ___ Love lift-ed me, ___
Love lift-ed e-ven me, Love lift-ed e-ven me, When noth-ing

Words: James Rowe (1865-1933)
Music: Howard E. Smith (1863-1918)

else could help, Love lift-ed me; ____ Love lift-ed me. ____

I Don't Feel No Ways Tired

I don't feel no ways tired, _____ I come too

far from where I start - ed from; __ No-bod - y

told me that the road would be eas - y, ____ I

don't be - lieve __ He brought me this far to leave me. ____

200

Stand by Me

Words: Charles A. Tindley (1851-1933)
Music: Charles A. Tindley; harm. F. A. Clark

1. rul - est wind   and wa - ter,
2. nev - er lost   a bat - tle,
3. know - est all   a - bout me,   Stand   by   me.   Stand   by   me.
4. saved   Paul   and Si - las,
5. "Lil - y   of   the Val - ley,"

I've Got Peace Like a River 201

1. I've   got   peace   like   a   riv - er,   I've   got   peace   like   a
2. I've   got   joy   like   a   foun - tain,   I've   got   joy   like   a
3. I've   got   love   like   an   o - cean,   I've   got   love   like   an

[1.]
1. riv - er,   I've   got   peace   like   a   riv - er   in   my
2. foun - tain,   I've   got   joy   like   a   foun - tain   in   my
3. o - cean,   I've   got   love   like   an   o - cean   in   my

[2.]
1. soul;   I've   got   riv - er   in   my   soul.
2. soul;   I've   got   foun - tain   in   my   soul.
3. soul;   I've   got   o - cean   in   my   soul.

Words: Traditional
Music: Negro Spiritual

1. The church of God must now prevail, against the world's divisive scheme; The mighty strength of Union pales, the adversary of the dream.

2. The church of God must now prevail, no breach deform its sacred walls; When storms of hate and doubt assail, let love and peace reign in its halls.

3. The love of God must now prevail, Christ spoke the love of Christ for all; And loving God, love cannot fail, to transcend ev'ry racial wall.

4. The peace of God must now prevail, in Christ shall wars and hatred end; The arms of earth cannot avail, the peace of heav'n alone can win.

5. The reign of God must now prevail,
Let selfish strivings be undone;
Across the world His name we hail,
Our Lord and King, the risen son!

There Is a Balm in Gilead

Words: Traditional
Music: American Melody; arr. Carl Haywood (b. 1949), from *The Haywood Collection of Negro Spirituals*,
Copyright © 1992.

Think of His Goodness to You

Words: R. C. Ward
Music: R. C. Ward

Trust and Obey

1. When we walk with the Lord In the light of His word, What a glo-ry He
2. Not a shad-ow can rise, Not a cloud in the skies, But His smile quick-ly
3. Not a bur-den we bear, Not a sor-row we share, But our toil He doth
4. But we nev-er can prove The de-lights of His love Un-til all on the
5. When in fel-low-ship sweet We will sit at His feet, Or we'll walk by His

1. sheds on our way! While we do His good will, He a-bides with us still,
2. drives it a-way; Not a doubt nor a fear, Not a sigh nor a tear,
3. rich-ly re-pay; Not a grief nor a loss, Not a frown nor a cross,
4. al-tar we lay; For the fav-or He shows, And the joy He be-stows,
5. side in the way; What He says we will do, Where He sends we will go,—

1. And with all who will trust and o-bey.
2. Can a-bide while we trust and o-bey.
3. But is blest if we trust and o-bey. Trust and o-bey, for there's
4. Are for them who will trust and o-bey.
5. Nev-er fear, on-ly trust and o-bey.

no oth-er way To be hap-py in Je-sus, But to trust and o-bey.

Words: J. H. Sammis
Music: D. B. Towner

We Walk By Faith

206

1. We walk by faith, and not by sight; no gra-cious words we hear from Him who spoke as none e'er spoke; but we be-lieve Him near.
2. We may not touch His hands and side, nor fol-low where He trod; but in His prom-ise we re-joice, and cry, "My Lord and God!"
3. Help then, O Lord, our un-be-lief; and may our faith a-bound, to call on you when you are near, and seek where you are found.
4. That, when our life of faith is done, in realms of clear-er light, we may be-hold you as you are, with full and end-less sight.

Words: Henry Alford (1810-1871)
Music: Eugene W. Hancock (b. 1929)
Music Copyright © 1992 Eugene W. Hancock

We'll Understand It Better By and By

1. We are of - ten tossed and driv'n on the rest - less sea of time,
2. We are of - ten des - ti - tude of the things that life de - mands,
3. Tri - als dark on ev - 'ry hand, and we can - not un - der - stand,
4. Temp - ta - tions, hid - den snares of - ten take us un - a - wares,

1. Som - ber skies and howl - ing tem - pest oft suc - ceed a bright sun - shine;
2. Want of food and want of shel - ter, thirst - y hills and bar - ren lands;
3. All the ways that God would lead us to that bless - ed prom - ised land;
4. And our hearts are made to bleed for many a thought - less word or deed;

1. In that land of per - fect day, when the mists have rolled a - way,
2. We are trust - ing in the Lord, and ac - cord - ing to His word,
3. But He guides us with His eye and we'll fol - low till we die.
4. And we won - der why the test when we try to do our best.

Words: Charles A. Tindley (1851-1933)
Music: Charles A. Tindley; arr. F. A. Clark, c. 1906

1. We will
2. We will
3. For we'll
4. But we'll

un - der-stand it bet - ter by and by, by and by.

By and by _____ when the morn-ing comes, When the saints of

God are gath - ered home, We'll tell the sto - ry

how we're o - ver - come; For we'll un - der - stand it bet - ter by and by, by and by.

We've Come This Far by Faith

Refrain

We've come this far — by — faith, Lean-ing on the Lord; — Trust-ing in His ho - ly word, He's nev-er failed — me yet. O _____

Fine

... can't turn a - round. __ We've come this far __ by __ faith. __

1. Don't be dis-cour-aged __ when trou-ble's __ in your life. He'll bear your

D.S.

bur - dens and move __ all mis - er- y and strife. That's why we've

2. Just the other day I heard someone say
He didn't believe in God's word;
But I can truly say that God had made a way
And He never failed me yet.
That's why we've (Refrain)

Yes, God Is Real

There are some things _____ I may not know, _____ these are some
plac - es I _____ can't go; _____ But I am sure _____ of this one
thing, _____ that God is real for I can feel Him deep with -

There are some things _____ I may not know, _____
There are plac - es I can't go; _____ But I am sure
of this one thing, _____ God is real He's

Down by the Riverside

1. Goin' to lay down my sword and shield,
2. Goin' to lay down my war ___ shoes,
3. Goin' to put on my long white robe,
4. Goin' to meet my lov - ing sav - ior,

Down by the riv-er-side, Down by the riv-er-side,

Down by the riv-er-side.
1. Goin' to lay down my sword and shield,
2. Goin' to lay down my war ___ shoes,
3. Goin' to put on my long white robe,
4. Goin' to meet my lov - ing sav - ior,

Down by the riv-er-side, To stud - y war ___ no

CHILDREN

Little David, Play on Your Harp

Lit-tle Da-vid, play on your harp, Hal - le - lu! Hal - le -
lu! Lit-tle Da-vid, play on your harp, Hal - le - lu! Lit-tle Da-vid. lu!

1. Lit - tle Da - vid was _____ a shep-herd boy, He
2. O _____ Josh-u - a was _____ the son of Nun, He

1. killed _____ Go - li - ath and _____ shout - ed for joy. _____
2. nev - er would quit _____ till the work _____ was done. _____

Words: Traditional
Music: Negro Spiritual

Words: Traditional, Jamaica
Music: Traditional, Jamaica; arr. Edward Henry
Copyright © 1981 Caribbean Conference of Churches

213

Children of the Heavenly Father

1. Chil - dren of the heav'n-ly Fa - ther Safe- ly in His bos - om gath - er;
2. God His own doth tend and nour - ish, In His ho - ly courts they flour - ish;
3. Nei - ther life nor death shall ev - er From the Lord His child-ren sev - er;
4. Praise the Lord in joy - ful num - bers, Your pro-tect-or nev - er slum - bers;
5. Though He giv - eth or He tak - eth, God His chil-dren ne'er for-sak - eth;

1. Nest-ling bird nor star in heav - en, Such a ref - uge e'er was giv - en.
2. From all e - vil things He spares them, In His might - y arms He bears them.
3. Un - to them His grace He show - eth, And their sor - rows all He know - eth.
4. At the will of your de - fend - er Ev - ery per - son must sur - ren - der.
5. His the lov - ing pur-pose sole - ly To pre - serve them pure and ho - ly.

Words: Carolina Sandell-Berg, 1855; tr. Ernst W. Olson, 1925
Music: Swedish Folk Melody
Text translation Copyright © Board of Publication, Lutheran Church in America. Reprinted by permission of
Augsburg Fortress.

214

God Is So Good

1. God is so good, God is so good,
2. He cares for me, He cares for me,
3. He's all I need, He's all I need,

1. God is so good, He's so good to me.
2. He cares for me, He's so good to me.
3. He's all I need, He's so good to me.

Words: Traditional
Music: Negro Spiritual

Great Are You, O Lord

215

3 part canon

1. God, our Fa - ther, we a - dore __ you, mag - ni - fy __ you;
2. Heav'n and earth pro - claim your pow - er, show your glo - ry;
3. Al - le - lu - ia, al - le - lu - ia, al - le - lu - ia;

1. God, our Fa - ther, we a - dore __ you, mag - ni - fy __ you;
2. Heav'n and earth pro - claim your pow - er, show your glo - ry;
3. Al - le - lu - ia, al - le - lu - ia, al - le - lu - ia;

Great are you, O Lord! _____

In My Life, Lord, Be Glorified

216

1. In my life, Lord, be glo - ri - fied, ___ be glo - ri - fied; ___
2. In my song, Lord, be glo - ri - fied, ___ be glo - ri - fied; ___
3. In your church, Lord, be glo - ri - fied, ___ be glo - ri - fied; ___

1. In my life, Lord, be glo - ri - fied ___ to - day.
2. In my song, Lord, be glo - ri - fied ___ to - day.
3. In your church, Lord, be glo - ri - fied ___ to - day.

He's Got the Whole World in His Hand

1. He's got the whole world in His hand, He's got the whole world in His hand, He's got the whole world in His hand, He's got the whole world in His hand.

2. He's got you and me sister, etc.
3. He's got you and me brother, etc.
4. He's got the pretty little baby, etc.
5. He's got everybody here, etc.

Words: Traditional
Music: Negro Spiritual; arr. Hezekiah Brinson, Jr. (b. 1958)

Jesus Loves Me, This I Know

1. Je - sus loves me! this I know, For the bi - ble tells me so;
2. Je - sus loves me! He who died, Hea - ven's gate to op - en wide;
3. Je - sus take this heart of mine, Make it pure and whol - ly thine;

1. Lit - tle ones to Him be - long; They are weak but He is strong.
2. He will wash a - way my sin, Let His lit - tle child come in.
3. On the cross you died for me, I will try to live for thee.

Yes, Je - sus loves me! ___ Yes, Je - sus loves me! ___

Yes, Je - sus loves me! ___ The bi - ble tells me so.

Words: Traditional; Anne B. Warner (1820-1915)
Music: William B. Bradbury (1816-1869); arr. Horace Clarence Boyer (b. 1935)
Arr. Copyright © 1992 Horace Clarence Boyer

This Is the Day

Words: Psalm 118:24
Music: Les Garrett

1. We are climb-ing Ja - cob's lad - der,
2. Ev' ry' round goes high - er, high - er,
3. Sin - ner do you love your Je - sus?
4. If you love Him why not serve Him,

1. We are climb-ing Ja - cob's lad - der;
2. Ev' ry' round goes high - er, high - er;
3. Sin - ner do you love your Je - sus?
4. If you love Him why not serve Him;

1. We are climb-ing Ja - cob's lad - der,
2. Ev' ry' round goes high - er, high - er,
3. Sin - ner do you love your Je - sus?
4. If you love Him why not serve Him,

1. Sol - diers of the cross.
2. Sol - diers of the cross.
3. Sol - diers of the cross.
4. Sol - diers of the cross.

Words: Traditional
Music: Negro Spiritual; arr. Horace Clarence Boyer (b. 1935)
Arr. Copyright © 1992 Horace Clarence Boyer

This Little Light of Mine

Words: Traditional
Music: Negro Spiritual; arr. Horace Clarence Boyer (b. 1935)
Arr. Copyright © 1992 Horace Clarence Boyer

1. shine,   let it   shine,   let it   shine. _____
2. shine,   let it   shine,   let it   shine. _____
3. shine,   let it   shine,   let it   shine. _____

Jesus Loves the Little Children 222

Je - sus loves the lit - tle chil - dren, All the chil - dren of the world; Red and yel - low, black and white, They are pre - cious in His sight, Je - sus loves the lit - tle chil - dren of the world.

Words: Anonymous
Music: George F. Root (1820-1895)

Words: Traditional
Music: Negro Spiritual; arr. Irma Tillery (b. 1925). Used by Permission.

Saul; Dere's none like good ole Josh - ua, an' de
bat - tle of Jer - i - cho. 2. Up to the walls of
Jer - i - cho, ___ He marched with spear in hand; "Go

D.C.

blow dem ram horns," Josh - ua cried, ___ "for the bat - tle am in my hand." Oh

Ezek'el Saw de Wheel

E-ze-k'el saw de wheel 'Way up in de mid-dle o' de air, E-ze-k'el saw de wheel 'Way in de mid-dle o' de air. De big wheel run by faith, De lit-tle wheel run by de Grace o' God, A wheel in a wheel __ 'Way in de mid-dle o' de air. __

Fine

1. Bet-ter min', my sis-ter, how you walk on de cross,
2. Let me tell you, broth-er, what a sin-ner will do, 'Way in de mid-dle o' de

D.C.

air, Yo' foot might slip an' yo' soul be los'. 'Way in de mid-dle o' de air. __
He'll step on you an' he'll step on me.

Words: Traditional
Music: Negro Spiritual; harm. J. Jefferson Cleveland (1937-1988)
Harm. Copyright © 1981 Abingdon. Reprinted from *Songs of Zion* by permission.

SOCIAL JUSTICE

Oh, Freedom!

1. Oh, free - dom! Oh, free - dom, Oh, free - dom o - ver me!
2. No mo' moan - in', no mo' moan - in', no mo' moan - in' o - ver me!

1. An' be fo' I'd be a slave I'll be bur - ied in my grave, An' go home to my Lord an' be free.
2. An' be fo' I'd be a slave I'll be bur - ied in my grave, An' go home to my Lord an' be free.

3. No mo' weepin'...
4. There'll be singin'...

5. There'll be shoutin'...
6. There'll be prayin'...

Words: Traditional
Music: Negro Spiritual; arr. Carl Haywood (b. 1949), from *The Haywood Collection of Negro Spirituals*,
Copyright © 1992.

Mine Eyes Have Seen the Glory

1. Mine___ eyes have seen the glo - ry of the
2. I have seen Him in the watch - fires of a
3. He has sound - ed forth the trum - et that shall
4. In the beau - ty of the lil - ies, Christ was

1. com - ing of the Lord; He is tram - pling out the vin - tage where the
2. hund - red cir - cling camps, They have build - ed Him an al - tar in the
3. nev - er sound re - treat, He is sift - ing out the hearts of men be -
4. born a - cross the sea, With a glo - ry in His bos - om that trans -

1. grapes of wrath are stored; He has loosed the fate - ful light - ning of His
2. eve - ning dews and damps; I can read His right - eous sent - ence by the
3. fore His judge - ment seat; O be swift, my soul, to an - swer Him! be
4. fig - ures you and me; As He died to make men ho - ly, let us

1. ter - ri - ble swift sword, His truth is march - ing on.
2. dim and flar - ing lamps, His day is march - ing on.
3. ju - bi - lant, my feet! Our God is march - ing on.
4. live to make all free, While God is march - ing on.

Words: Jula W. Howe (1819-1910)
Music: *Battle Hymn of the Republic*, William Steffe; arr. Horace Clarence Boyer (b. 1935)
Arr. Copyright © 1992 Horace Clarence Boyer

Glo - ry, glo - ry, hal - le - lu - jah!

Glo - ry, glo - ry, hal - le - lu - jah! Glo - ry, glo - ry, hal - le

lu - jah! His truth is march - ing on.

We Shall Overcome

We shall o-ver-come,____ We shall o-ver come,____ we shall o-ver-come some - day;____ Oh,____ deep in my heart,____ I do be - lieve,____ (Oh)

1.- 4. We shall o-ver-come some - day.____ **5.** day.

2. We'll walk hand in hand, today.
3. God is on our side, today.
4. We are not afraid, today.
5. We shall live in peace, someday.

1. When Is - rael was in E-gypt's land, let my peo - ple go;
2. The Lord told Mo - ses what to do, let my peo - ple go;
3. They jour-neyed on at his com - mand, let my peo - ple go;
4. Oh, let us all from bond-age flee, let my peo - ple go;

1. op - pressed so hard they __ could not stand, let my peo - ple go.
2. to lead the chil-dren of Is - rael through, let my peo - ple go.
3. and came at length to __ Ca-naan's land, let my peo - ple go.
4. and let us all in __ Christ be free, let my peo - ple go.

Go down, __ Mo - ses, way down in E- gypt's land; __

tell old Pha - raoh to let my peo - ple go.

Words: Traditional
Music: Negro Spiritual; arr. Horace Clarence Boyer (b. 1935)
Arr. Copyright © 1992 Horace Clarence Boyer

Mar-tin's dream for all of us so set his soul a - fire, ____ And lift - ed him to soar - ing heights that he might with his God con - spire; ____ To change the course of his - to - ry that all be bro-thers, all be free. Keep the dream a - live, _____ Keep the dream a -

live; _____ We will have the vic - to - ry, Just

1.
keep the dream a - live. __ We'll

2.
keep the dream a - live.

We will

Free at Last 230

Free at last, free at last, I thank God I'm

free at last, Free at last, free at last, _____

Words: Traditional
Music: Negro Spiritual; arr. John W. Work (1901-1967)
Arr. used by permission of Mrs. J. W. Work.

I thank God I'm free at last. O free at last.

1. 'Way __ down yon- der in the grave - yard walk, I thank God I'm
2. On - a my knees __ when the light pass'd by, I thank God I'm
3. Some of these morn - ings, __ bright and fair, I thank God I'm

1. free at last, _____ Me and my Je - sus goin' to
2. free at last, _____ Tho't __ my soul ____ would __
3. free at last, Goin' meet __ King Je - sus ____

1. meet and talk, _____ I thank God I'm free at last, O
2. rise and fly, _____ I thank God I'm free at last, O
3. in the air, _____ I thank God I'm free at last, ____

BENEDICTION

A Choral Benediction

The Lord bless you and keep you: The Lord make his

face to shine upon you, And be

And be

gra-cious un-to you, The Lord lift up His coun-te-nance up-on

you, And give you peace. A -

A -

A -

Words: Numbers 6:24-26
Music: Carl Haywood (b. 1949), from *Songs of Praise*, Copyright ©1992.

men, A - men, A - men.

232

Thank You, Lord

Thank you, Lord, _____ Thank _____ you, _____

Lord; _____ Thank _____ you, _____ Lord _____

I just want to thank you, _ Lord. _____

Words: Traditional
Music: Negro Spiritual; arr. Hezekiah Brinson, Jr. (b. 1958)
Arr. Copyright © 1990 Hezekiah Brinson, Jr. All Rights Reserved.

Amen

A - men, A - men,
Lord - y   good Lord - y
1. See the lit - tle ba - by
A - men, A - men, A - men,

1. Ly - ing in a man - ger   On __ Christ - mas morn - ing.
2. Talk-ing to the eld- ers,   They __ mar-v'ld at His wis - dom.
3. Pray-ing to his fa - ther   As __ Ju - das be-trays Him.
4. Dy - ing for us sin -ners   but He rose __ on __ Eas - ter.

A - men, A - men,

1.,2.,3.   **4.**

2. See Him   in the tem - ple,
3. See Him   in the gar- den,
4. See Him there at Cal-v'ry,

A - men, A - men, A - men.   men.

Words: Traditional
Music: Negro Spiritual; arr. Horace Clarence Boyer (b. 1935)
Arr. Copyright © 1992 Horace Clarence Boyer

God Be With You

God _____ be with you, _____ God _____ be

with you, _____ God _____ be with you, _____ un-til we

meet ____ a - gain; ____ God _____ be with you,

God _____ be with you, _____ God _____ be

with you, _____ un - til we meet a - gain. _____

Words: Thomas A. Dorsey (1899-1993)
Music: Tomas A. Dorsey; arr. Horace Clarence Boyer (b. 1935)
Words and Music Copyright © 1940 Unichappell Music, Inc. (BMI). Copyright renewed, assigned to Chappell & Co.
International Copyright Secured. All Rights Secured.

Service Music

KYRIE

235

Lord, Have Mercy

Lord have mer - cy, Lord have mer - cy, Lord have mer - cy.

Christ have mer - cy,

Christ have __ mer - cy, Christ __ have __ mer- cy.

Lord, Have Mercy

236

Lord, have mer - cy, Lord, have

mer - cy, Lord, have ner - cy on

us. _____ Christ, have

mer - cy, Christ, have mer - cy,

Christ, have mer - cy on us. _____

Lord, have mer - cy,

Lord, have mer - cy, Lord, have

mer - cy, have mer - cy on us.

Music: Avon Gillespie (1937-1989), *Mass No. 1 in G*

Music: William B. Cooper

Kyrie Eleison

Lord, Have Mercy

Lord, _____ have mer - cy, Have mer - cy, have mer - cy! Lord, __

_____ have mer - cy, Have mer - cy, have mer - cy. __ Lord,

_____ have mer - cy, Have mer - cy, have mer - cy! Lord, __

_____ have mer - cy. _____

GLORIA

Glory to God 241

Glo-ry to God in the high-est, and peace to His peo-ple on earth. Lord God, heav-en-ly King, al-might-y God and Fa-ther,

Music: David Hurd (b. 1950), *Intercession Mass*

Lord God, Lamb of God, you take a - way the sin of the
Sw.
Man.

world: have mer-cy on us;
Gt.
Sw.
Gt.
Ped.

you are seat-ed at the right hand of the Fa - ther: re - ceive our

prayer.
For
Gt.

Glory to God

Leader Glo-ry to God in the high-est, *All* And ___ peace ___ to His peo-ple on earth. Lord ___ God, heav'n-ly ___ King, Al - migh-ty God, and Fa - ther, ___ we wor-ship you, we give you thanks, we praise you for your glo - - ry.

Music: Lena McLin, *Eucharist of the Soul*
Reprinted from *Eucharist of the Soul* (GC41)
Copyright © 1972 General Words and Music Co., San Diego, CA. Reprinted with permission 1993.

Lord Je-sus Christ, on-ly Son of the Fa-ther, Lord God, Lamb of God, you

take a-way the sin of the world: have mer-cy __ on us;

You are seat-ed at the right hand of the Fa-ther: __ re-ceive __

__ our prayer. For you a-lone are the

Ho- ly One,   you a- lone are the Lord,   you a-

lone are the Most High, Je - sus Christ, with the Ho - ly Spir - it, in the

glo-ry of God _ the Fa - ther. A - men. A -

men.   A - men. A - men.

1. Glo-ry to God __ in the high - est and peace to His peo - ple on earth. __

2. Lord God, heav-en-ly King, al - might-y God and Fa - ther, we

wor-ship you, __ we give you thanks, __ we praise you for __ your glo - ry.

Unison

3. Lord Je-sus Christ, on-ly son of the Fa - ther, Lord God, Lamb of God, Glo-ry,

Glo-ry, hal-le-lu - jah, Lord we praise your Ho - ly name, ___ Glo-ry,

Glo-ry ha-le-lu - jah, Lord we praise your Ho - ly name. ___ 4. You

Unison

7. You a-lone — are the Most High, Je - sus Christ, with the Ho - ly Spi-rit, in the

Descant

Lord, ———— Lord — we

glo-ry of — the Fa - ther. Glo-ry, Glo-ry, hal-le-lu - jah, Lord we

praise ———— you ———— Lord, ———— Lord — hal - le -

praise your Ho - ly name, — Glo-ry, Glo-ry ha-le-lu - jah, Lord we

SONGS OF PRAISE

I Will Rejoice

I will re-joice, _____ I will be glad, _

I will praise God Who holds _ my life, _

Words: Grayson Warren Brown (b. 1948)
Music: Grayson Warren Brown; harm. Larry Adams

in __ His hands. _____ I will re-joice,

1. I will praise the Fa - ther, _____
2. I will praise the Fa - ther, _____

1. I will praise the Son. _____   I will praise the Spir -
2. each and ev' - ry day _____   and I will sing His love _

1. - it for - ev - er more. _____ I will re - joice,_
2. _ songs for - ev - er more. _____ I will re - joice,_

1. _____ I will be glad, _____
2. _____ I will be glad, _____

I will praise God, Who holds_ my life _ in _ His hands. _

D.S.

D.S.

We Have Come Into His House

Praise, praise, hon - or and glo - ry, Praise, praise,

hon - or and glo - ry, Hon - or and glo - ry to Christ, our King.

PRAYERS OF THE PEOPLE AND RESPONSES

The Prayers of the People: Form I

Leader

With all our heart and with all our mind, let us pray to the Lord,

Say - ing "Lord, have _ mer - cy.

Leader

* For . . . . , let us pray to the Lord.

People

Lord, have _ mer - cy.

(This response is sung after each petition)

Leader Concludes

In the communion of [_____ and of all the] saints, let us commend

ourselves, and one an- o- ther, and all our life, to Christ our God.

People

To thee, / you, O Lord our God. A - men.

The complete text is located in The Book of Common Prayer.

Music: Carl Haywood (b. 1949), from *Mass for Grace*, Copyright © 1992.

Leader:

Let us pray for the Church and for the world.

Grant, Almighty God, that all who confess your Name may be united in your
    truth, live together in your love, and reveal your glory in the world. *Response*

Guide the people of this land, and of all the nations, in the ways of justice
    and peace; that we may honor one another and serve the common good. *Response*

Give us all a reverence for the earth as your own creation, that we may use
    its resources rightly in the service of others and to your honor and glory. *Response*

Bless all whose lives are closely linked with ours, and grant that
    we may serve Christ in them, and love one another as he loves us. *Response*

Comfort and heal all those who suffer in body, mind, or spirit; give them
    courage and hope in their troubles, and bring them the joy of your salvation. *Response*

We commend to your mercy all who have died, that your will for them may
    be fulfilled; and we pray that we may share with all your saints in your eternal kingdom.
                                                      Response

Response

Leader   *People*

(silence)

Lord, in your mer-cy,   Hear our prayer.

Hear our prayer, O Lord, hear our prayer, O Lord; In-

cline thine ear to us, and grant us thy peace.

Words: George Whelpton (1847-1930)
Music: George Whelpton

O Lord, Hear us, we pray.

Words: James E. Moore, Jr.
Music: James E. Moore, Jr.

Lead me, Lord, _____ lead me in thy right - eous-ness, _____
Make thy way plain be - fore thy face. A - men.

Words: Psalm 5:8, 4:8
Music: Samuel S. Wesley (1861-1935)

SANCTUS

252

Holy, Holy, Holy

Ho - ly, ho - ly, ly, _____

Holy, Holy, Holy

God of pow - er and might,

1. Heav - en and earth____ are full_____
2.,3. Bless - ed is he_____ who comes_____

1. of your glo - ry.
2.3. in the name of the Lord.

1.,2.

Ho - san - na!_____ Ho - san -

na _____ in the high -

est. _____ san - na, _____ Ho -

san - na _____ in the high - est.

Holy, Holy, Holy

Ho - ly, Ho - ly, Ho - ly Lord,

God of pow - er and might,

Heav - en and earth are full of your

glo - ry._____ Ho - san - na in_____ the

high-est. Bless- ed is he who

comes in the name of the Lord. Ho - san - na

in_____ the high-est._____

Ho - ly, ho - ly, _____ ho - ly, ho - ly, _____ ho - ly Lord God _____ of hosts. _____

Heav - en and earth ___ are ___ filled with your glo -

ry. Ho - san - na in ___ the ___ high - est. ___

Bless - ed is ___ He who ___ comes in the name ___

of the Lord, _____ of the Lord. _____

Ho - san - na _____ in the high -

est, ho - san - na in ___ the ___ high - est. _____

Holy, Holy, Holy

Leader

(piano) Ho - ly,

Ho - ly, ho - ly, ho - ly Lord, God of pow'r __ and might, heav - en and earth are full of your glo - ry. Ho - san - na in the high - est. Bless - ed is he who comes in the name of the Lord. Ho - san - na in the high - est. ___

MEMORIAL ACCLAMATION

Therefore We Proclaim the Mystery of Faith   257

There-fore we pro - claim _ the mys - ter - y of faith; _____

Christ ___ has died. _____ Christ ___ is ri - sen. ____ Christ will come a- gain al - le - lu - ia! _____

Christ Has Died

Christ has died. Christ is ris-en. __ Christ will come a-gain.

Music: Marjorie Gabriel-Burrow
Copyright © 1992 G.I.A. Publications, Inc., Chicago, IL. All Rights Reserved.

Christ Has Died

Leader
Christ __ has died.

Christ has died. __

Christ is ris-en. Christ will come __ a-gain.

Music: Betty Carr Pulkingham (b. 1928), *Freedom Mass.* Based on traditional African melodies.
Copyright © 1975 CELEBRATION (Administered by MARANATHA! MUSIC c/o The Copyright Company,
Nashville, TN). All Rights Reserved. International Copyright Secured. Used by Permission.

We Remember His Death

We re-mem-ber His death,___ We pro-claim His re-su-rect-ion,___ We a-wait___ His com - ing___ in glo - ry._____ We re-glo - ry. We re-glo - ry.___

AMEN

Amen

Amen

THE LORD'S PRAYER

263

The Lord's Prayer

Our Fa - ther in heav - en, hal - lowed be your Name, your king-dom come, your will be done, on earth as in heav - en. Give us to - day our dai - ly bread. For - give us our sins as we for - give those — who sin a - gainst us. ____ Save us

from the time of trial, ____ and de - li - ver us from e - vil. _

For the king - dom, the pow - er, and the glo - ry are

yours, now and for - ev - er. ____ A - men. ____

The Lord's Prayer

Music: Carl Haywood (b. 1949), from *Mass for Grace*, Copyright © 1992.

give those who sin a-gainst us. Save us from the time of tri - al, and de -

liv - er us from e - vil. For the king - dom, the pow - er, and the

glo - ry are yours, now and for - ev - er. A - men.

done, on ___ earth ___ as in heav - en. Give us to-day
those who ___ sin ___ a - gainst us. Save ___ us _

done, on ___ earth as in heav - en.
those, those who sin ___ a - gainst ___ us.

power, and the glo - ry are yours, now and for - ev -

power, and the glo - ry are yours,

- er, ___ A - men.

now and for - ev - er. A - men.

The Lord's Prayer

Our Fa - ther, __ who are in hea - ven, _____

hal - lowed be thy Name, Thy king - dom come, Thy will be

done, _____ on earth as it is in hea - ven. _____

Give us __ this day our __ dai - ly bread. For - give us ___ our tres - pass -

Music: Garfield Rochard

es, As we — for-give those who tres - pass — a-gainst us,

as we for - give, And lead us not in - to temp -

ta - tion, __ but de - li - ver us from e - vil. __ And lead us

not in - to temp - ta - tion, __ but de - li - ver us from e - vil.

FRACTION ANTHEMS

268

Christ Our Passover

Al-le - lu - ia, Al - le - lu - ia, Al - le - lu - ia.

Leader

Christ our pass-o-ver is sac-ri - ficed _ for us;

Response

(organ)

There - fore let _ us _ keep the

Lamb of God

Lamb of __ God, you take a - way the sins of the world: have mer-cy on us.

Lamb of __ God, you take a - way the

sins of the world: have mer-cy on us.

Lamb of __ God, you take __ a-way the

sins __ of the world: grant _____ us _____ peace.

Lamb of God

Lamb of

God, you take a - way the sins of the

world: have mer - cy on us. Lamb of

God, you take a - way the sins of the

Music: Marjorie Landsmark-DeLewis (b. 1930)
Copyright © August 1990 Marjorie Landsmark-DeLewis

world: have   mer -   cy   on   us. _____   Lamb   of

God,   you   take __ a -   way   the __ sins __ of   the

world: _____   grant __ us __ peace. _____

Lamb of God

mer - cy on us.　Lamb of God, you take a-way the sins of the world:

grant us peace. _____

Do This in Remembrance of Me

1. Do this in re-mem-brance of me.
2. Eat this in re-mem-brance of me.
3. Drink this in re-mem-brance of me.

1. Do this in re-mem-brance of me.
2. Eat this in re-mem-brance of me.
3. Drink this in re-mem-brance of me.

I hung out on a tree

Music: Glenn Burleigh

for thee, _____ for thee, _____

1. Do   this   in re - mem - brance of me. _____
2. Eat   this   in re - mem - brance of me. _____
3. Drink this   in re - mem - brance of me.

PSALMS

Refrain: **His Love Is Everlasting**

Suggested Use: Easter, General

His love, _____ His love, _____ His love _____ is ev - er - last - ing. _____

Psalm 126

1. When the Lord restored the fortunes of **Zi**on,*
   then were we like those who **dream.**

2. Then was our mouth filled with **laugh**ter,*
   and our tongue with shouts of **joy.**   *Refrain*

3. Then they said among the **na**tions,*
   "The Lord has done great things for **them.**"

4. The Lord has done great things for **us,***
   and we are glad in**deed.**

† 5. Restore our fortunes, O **Lord,***
   like the watercourses of the **Ne**gev.   *Refrain*

6. Those who sowed with **tears***
   will reap with songs of **joy.**

7. Those who go out weeping, carrying the **seed,***
   will come again with joy, shouldering their **sheaves.** *Refrain*

   † (repeat second half of chant)

Suggested Use: Easter, General

Psalm 145: 8-13

8. The Lord is gracious and full of com**pas**sion,*
   slow to anger and of great **kind**ness.

9. The Lord is loving to **every**one*
   and his compassion is over all his **works**.   *Refrain*

10. All your works praise you, O **Lord**,*
    and your faithful servants **bless** you.

11. They make known the glory of your **king**dom*
    and speak of your **pow**er;   *Refrain*

12. That the peoples may know of your **pow**er*
    and the glorious splendor of your **king**dom.

13. Your kingdom is an everlasting **king**dom;*
    your dominion endures throughout all **ages**.   *Refrain*

Refrain: Leon C. Roberts (1950-1999). Refrain: © 1987 Leon Roberts.
Simplified Anglican Chant: Robert Knox Kennedy. Chant used by permission.

Refrain: **Lord, Send Out Your Spirit**

Suggested Use: Pentecost, Rogation Days

Lord, send out your spir - it! _____

Lord, send out your spir - it! _____

until **Final ending**

Lord, send out your spir - it! And re - new the face of the earth.

Refrain: Rawn Harbor (b. 1947). Used by Permission.
Simplified Anglican Chant: Jerome Webster Meachen. Permission Requested.

Psalm 104: 25-26, 28-32, 35

25. O Lord, how manifold are your **works**!*
    in wisdom you have made them all; the earth is full of your **crea**tures.
26. Yonder is the great and wide sea with its living things too many to **num**ber,*
    creatures both small and **great**. *Refrain*
28. All of them look to **you***
    to give them their food in due **sea**son.
29. You give it to them; they **gath**er it;*
    you open your hand, and they are filled with good **things**. *Refrain*
30. You hide your face, and they are **ter**rified;*
    you take away their breath, and they die and return to their **dust**.
31. You send forth your Spirit, and they are cre**ated;***
    and so you renew the face of the **earth**. *Refrain*
32. May the glory of the Lord endure for**ever**;*
    may the Lord rejoice in all his **works**.
35. May these words of mine **please** him;*
    I will rejoice in the **Lord**. *Refrain*

Refrain: **My God, Why Have You Abandoned Me?**

Suggested Use: Palm Sunday, Good Friday

My God,   my God,   why have you a -

ban - doned   me? _____

Refrain: Rawn Harbor (b. 1947). Used by Permission.
Simplified Anglican Chant: Carl Haywood (b. 1949), from *Mass for Grace*, Copyright © 1992.

Psalm 22: 1-2, 7-8, 14-21

1. My God, My God, why have youe for**sak**en me?*
   and are so far from my cry and from the words of my dis**tress**?
2. O my God, I cry in the daytime, but you do not **an**swer;*
   by night as well, but I find no **rest**.
7. All who see me laugh me to **scorn**;*
   they curl their lips and wag their heads, **say**ing,
8. "He trusted in the Lord; let him de**liv**er him;*
   let him rescue him, if he de**lights** in him." *Refrain*
14. I am poured out like water; all my bones are out of **joint**;*
    my heart within my breast is melting **wax**.
15. My mouth is dried out like a pot-sherd;
    my tongue sticks to the roof of my **mouth**;*
    and you have laid me in the dust of the **grave**. *Refrain*
16. Packs of dogs close me in, and gangs of evildoers circle a**round** me;*
    they pierce my hands and my feet; I can count my **bones**.
17. They stare and gloat **over** me;*
    they divide my garments among them; they cast lots for my **cloth**ing.
18. Be not far away, O **Lord**;*
    you are my strength; hasten to **help** me.
19. Save me from the **sword**,*
    my life from the power of the **dog**. *Refrain*
20. Save me from the lion's **mouth**,*
    my wretched body from the horns of wild **bulls**.
21. I will declare your Name to my **breth**ren;*
    in the midst of the congregation I will **praise** you. *Refrain*

Refrain: **The Lord Is My Light and My Salvation**

Suggested Use: Epiphany, General

The Lord is my light and my sal - va - tion.

Psalm 27: 1-9

1. The Lord is my light and my salvation; whom then'shall I'fear?*
   the Lord is the strength of my life; of whom then'shall I'be a'fraid?

2. When evildoers came upon me to eat'up my'flesh,*
   it was they, my foes and my'adversaries, who'stumbled and'fell. *Refrain*

3. Though an army should en'camp a'gainst me,*
   yet my'heart shall not'be a'fraid;

4. And though war should rise'up a'gainst me,*
   yet will I'put my'trust in'Him. *Refrain*

5. One thing have I asked of the Lord;'one thing I'seek;*
   that I may dwell in the house of the'Lord all the'days of my'life;

6. To behold the fair'beauty of the'Lord*
   and to'seek him'in his'temple. *Refrain*

7. For in the day of trouble he shall keep me'safe in his'shelter;*
   he shall hide me in the secrecy of his dwelling
   and set me'high up'on a'rock.

8. Even now he lifts'up my'head*
   above my'enemies'round a'bout me.

9. Therefore I will offer in his dwelling an oblation
   with'sounds of great'gladness;*
   I will sing and make'music'to the'Lord. *Refrain*

Refrain: **Serve the Lord With Gladness, Alleluia**

Suggested Use: Easter, General

Serve the Lord with glad - ness, al - le - lu - ia.

(organ)

Psalm 100: 1-4

1. O be joyful in the 'Lord all ye 'lands;*
    serve the Lord with gladness
    and come before his 'presence' with a 'song.   *Refrain*

2. Be ye sure that the Lord he is God;
    it is he that hath made us and not 'we our 'selves;*
    we are his' people and the' sheep of his' pasture.   *Refrain*

3. O go your way into his gates with thanksgiving
    and into his' courts with' praise;*
    be thankful unto' him and speak' good of his' Name.   *Refrain*

4. For the Lord is gracious;
    his mercy is' ever' lasting;*
    and his truth endureth from gener' ation to' gener' ation.   *Refrain*

Soprano descant (after Verse 4)

Al - le - lu - ia, al - le - lu - ia.

Refrain: David Hurd (b. 1950). Copyright © David Hurd. Used by Permission.
Anglican Chant: Henry Walford Davies, Permission Requested.

Suggested Use: Lent, Easter, Baptism, Burial

Psalm 23

1. The Lord is my **shep**herd;*
   I shall not **want**.
2. He maketh me to lie down in green **pas**tures;*
   he leadeth me beside the still **wa**ters. *Refrain*
3. He restoreth my **soul**;*
   he leadeth me in the paths of righteousness for His Name's **sake**.
4. Yea, though I walk through the valley of the shadow of death,
   I will fear no **evil**;*
   for thou are with me; thy rod and thy staff they **com**fort me. *Refrain*
5. Thou preparest a table before me in the presence of mine **en**emies;*
   thou anointest my head with oil; my cup runneth **over**.
6. Surely goodness and mercy shall follow me all the days of my **life**,*
   and I will dwell in the house of the Lord for**ever**. *Refrain*

Refrain: Leon C. Roberts (1950-1999). Refrain: © 1987 Leon Roberts.
Simplified Anglican Chant: Robert Knox Kennedy. Chant used by permission.

Refrain: **To You, O Lord**
Suggested Use: Advent, Ascension

To you, O Lord, I lift up my

soul, _____ to on-ly you, O Lord;

I wait for your re - turn.

Psalm 24: 1-10

1. The earth is the Lord's and all that is **in** it,*
   the world and all who dwell there**in**.

2. For it is he who founded it upon the **seas**
   and made it firm upon the rivers of the **deep**. *Refrain*

3. "Who can ascend the hill of the **Lord**?*
   and who can stand in his holy **place**?"

4. "Those who have clean hands and a pure **heart**,*
   who have not pledged themselves to falsehood,
   nor sworn by what is a **fraud**. *Refrain*

5. They shall receive a blessing from the **Lord**
   and a just reward from the God of their sal**va**tion."

6. Such is the generation of those who seek **him**,*
   of those who seek your face, O God of **Jac**ob. *Refrain*

7. Lift up your heads, O gates; lift them high, O everlasting **doors**;*
   and the King of glory shall come **in**.

8. "Who is this King of **glory**?"*
   "The Lord, strong and mighty, the Lord, mighty in **bat**tle." *Refrain*

9. Lift up your heads, O gates; lift them high, O everlasting **doors**;*
   and the King of glory shall come **in**.

10. "Who is He, this King of **glory**?"*
    "The Lord of hosts, he is the King of **glo**ry." *Refrain*

Prayer for Africa

English 1. Bless, O Lord, our coun-try, Af - ri - ca. So that she may wak - en
Swahili 2. Bwa-na, i - ba - ri - ki Af - ri - ka, I - li - i - pa - te _____
Zulu 3. Nko - si si - kel - el' i Af - ri - ka, Mal - u - pa-kam' u - pon-

from her sleep. Fill her horn with plen - ty, guide her feet.
ku - am - ka. Ma - om - bi ye ta ya - si - ki - lel.
do - lway - o; Yi - va im - i - tan - da - zo ye - tu.

Hear us, faith - ful ones Spir - it, de - scend, (Spir - it, Spir - it.)
U - tu - ba - ri - ki. U - je Ro-ho, (U - je, U - je.)
U - si - si-kel-el - e, Yih - la Moy-a, (Yih - la Mo-ya.)

Spir - it, de-scend, Spir - it, de-scend, Spir - it di - vine.
U - je Ro-ho. U - je Ro-ho. U - tu - ja - ze.
Yih - la Moy-a. Oy - ing cwel - e.

Words: Zula-Enoch Sontonga; English, Katherine F. Rohrbough
Music: Enoch Sontonga

Indices

Indices

Composers, Harmonizers, Arrangers, and Sources for Hymns

Composers, Harmonizers, Arrangers, and Sources for Hymns   375

Authors, Translators, and Sources for Hymns

Composers, Arrangers, and Sources for Service Music

TITLES & First Lines